SELF-HYPNOSIS FOR THE 21ST CENTURY

Create Your Eight-Step Personal Change Blueprint

Debbie Taylor

Self-Hypnosis for the 21st Century
Create Your Eight-Step Personal Change Blueprint
Debbie Taylor

Copyright © 2022 Debbie Taylor
All Rights Reserved.

Book Cover Design by Pankaj Singh Renu

Edited by www.TamelyndaLux/editing.com

All rights reserved. No part of this publication may be reproduced, distributed, or transmitted in any form or by any means, including photocopying, recording, or other electronic or mechanical methods, without prior written permission from the author, except in the case of brief quotations embodied in critical reviews and certain other non-commercial uses permitted by copyright law.

Disclaimer - Names, characters, businesses, events, and incidents are the products of the author's imagination. Any resemblance to actual persons, living or dead, or actual events is purely coincidental.

The information in this book, including any links to hypnosis recordings or PDFs, is NOT meant to replace medical or psychological treatment or consultation. If you have a serious medical condition, please consult with your physician.

Portions of this book have been previously published.

Self-Hypnosis for the 21st Century

Create Your Eight-Step Personal Change Blueprint

Debbie Taylor

debbietaylor-author.com

ISBN 978-1-7367549-1-7

First Printing June 2022

Debbie Taylor

Intuitive Life Coach LLC

Portland, Oregon

intuitivelifecoachpublishing.com

Debbie Taylor is available to speak at your business conference event on a variety of topics. Call 503-312-4660 for booking information.

Why Read This Book?

Got any bad habits you want to get rid of? Of course you do; you're human! Wouldn't it be great if you could train your brain to wake up on time every morning, be fully awake, and ready to go? How about training yourself to go to a party where you are able to enjoy *one* single drink and be content with that? How would it be if you could create the habit of picking things up around the house and keeping them put away on a regular basis? How would your life improve if you could train your brain to stick to a schedule, a routine, a way of life that would just make everything run smoothly? You can do all that and more with self-hypnosis.

Skip the hypno-jargon and learn to practice self-hypnosis easily and effectively by creating your Personal Change Blueprint. By understanding how the mind works and how hypnosis works, you can create daily habits that support you instead of frustrate you. Hypnosis isn't mystical or magical; it is science. In this book, you will learn the basics of the science behind hypnosis and habit change.

By applying what I teach you in this book, you can train yourself to do anything and everything you want. Where do you want to start? You can do it all with self-hypnosis.

By creating a consistent practice of self-hypnosis, you can train yourself to . . .

- Stop procrastinating
- Save money
- Quit smoking
- Lose weight
- Sleep through the night
- Stop worrying
- Love exercising
- Be present

Other Books by Debbie Taylor

Mastering the Law of Attraction: Your Personal Change Blueprint

Mastering the Law of Attraction to Manifest Financial Abundance: Your Personal Change Blueprint

Debbie has artfully combined her unique understanding of hypnosis and the Law of Attraction. She has put it all together in several easy-to-understand formats from which everyone can learn.

Written by a leading expert with over thirty years of experience as a hypnotist, life coach, teacher, online course creator, and author specializing in helping others create phenomenal life transformations.

As a retired educator and administrator in both the public and private sectors, Debbie has spent her life teaching others how to create real, permanent change in all areas of life. Combining her skill and love of hypnosis with her eight-step Personal Change Blueprint, Debbie has discovered the recipe for self-hypnosis that works every time.

In this book, Debbie teaches the reader how to do self-hypnosis. She explains why we do the things we do and how the practice of self-hypnosis can lead to positive long-term change.

Do you want Debbie Taylor to be the motivational speaker at your next event?

Call 503-312-4660 or email Debbie at dtaylor@debbietaylor-author.com

Debbie's ability to explain the mechanics of the conscious and subconscious mind makes for an informative and entertaining experience for all attendees. Audience members are captivated as they learn not only how they acquire the subconscious programs that result in daily habits, rituals, and routines but how they can put themselves in the driver's seat of the subconscious mind to eliminate unwanted thoughts and habits in exchange for the satisfaction of taking control of their lives in every area.

What others are saying about this book

"This book is amazing! The process Debbie teaches in this book will blow you away, and I know what I'm talking about. The Personal Change Blueprint is an amazing work of art that leaves other hypnotists shaking their heads and wishing they had come up with it first. There are countless books on self-hypnosis, but this one is the very best, by far. Your life will be better because of this book!"

Dr. Richard Nongard,
Author of *The Seven Most Effective Methods of Self-Hypnosis*

"Self-hypnosis for the 21st Century is outstanding! Debbie Taylor delivers the "how-to" so anyone can rapidly learn and apply self-hypnosis in any area, including weight loss, smoking, or procrastination. Her *Eight Step Personal Change Blueprint* guarantees success in designing and implementing your personal self-hypnosis program. If you have struggled learning self-hypnosis in the past, Taylor's process ensures a winning experience."

Linda Wells, Ed.D.,
Educator and Hypnotist

"This book far exceeded my expectations. As a therapeutic hypnotist and hypnosis trainer, I honestly thought that I had read everything worthwhile on the topic of self-hypnosis. Having read *Self-hypnosis for the 21st Century*, I now realize how wrong I was.

Debbie Taylor writes from a place of experience and expertise. That much is clear from page one. This book will teach you how to practice self-hypnosis easily, removing any unnecessary hurdles or unhelpful mysteries. Yet, as a testament to the quality of writing here, the sense of magic surrounding this life-changing practice remains.

Taylor shares theory and practice in perfect ratio, inspiring and educating the reader as to the very real life-changing potential of self-hypnosis. Even if you are well-acquainted with hypnosis and the process of self-hypnosis, I am convinced you will find immense value in this book. The Personal Change Blueprint is a therapeutic work of art that is both more powerful and more useful than it may seem. I fully intend to utilize the blueprint in self-hypnosis, therapy sessions, and beyond.

Grab this insightful book and begin implementing its lessons at your earliest opportunity. You will be glad you did!

Graham Old, Solution-focused Therapist and
Author of *How to do Hypnosis*

"Almost everyone wants change, but not everyone has the time or financial resources to afford to use a professional hypnotist to help them. Debbie Taylor has the solution.

She outlines a deceptively easy system to make lasting changes to your life using her Personal Change Blueprint, a system that takes just minutes a day. Minutes you can easily find in your day, even if it is while lounging in the tub or waiting for the kids at sports practice.

Debbie shows just how easy and simple it is to take yourself into a hypnotic state and, from there, to change your life through thought and repetition. She makes abundantly clear how the subconscious mind cannot differentiate between actions and facts vs. thoughts and fiction and teaches you how to deftly use this fact to create the changes you wish to make.

As a bonus, she models using the Blueprint to stop procrastination, end testing anxiety, lose weight, get rid of insomnia, and stop smoking. By the end of the book, you will be a pro at writing your own Personal Change Blueprint and using self-hypnosis to make the changes you so desire."

Sherene Silverberg,
Professional Hypnotist

"Great resource! Debbie Taylor dives deep with this self-help book as she teaches how and why self-hypnosis works. She even answers common questions and then skillfully details many other answers to questions you may not have thought to ask. You cannot go wrong with this in your library. I highly recommend it to everyone.

> Eva Wells, Hypnosis Instructor and
> Author of *Rejuvenate Your Life*

Table of Contents

Introduction i
How to Get the Most Out of this Book iii

SECTION ONE: Self-Hypnosis is Easy 1

Chapter One: How to Practice Self-Hypnosis 3
- Creating the Right Environment 4
- Plan Ahead 5
- Your Focus 6

Chapter Two: The Process 9
- What It Looks Like When I Practice Self-Hypnosis 13

Chapter Three: Common Questions About "Doing" Self-Hypnosis 17

SECTION TWO: Neural Pathways and How the Subconscious Mind Works 23

Chapter Four: It Is All About Neural Pathways 25
Chapter Five: Where Do Neural Pathways Come From? 33
- Conscious Mind and Subconscious Mind 35
- The Critical Faculty 36
- Brainwave States 41

Chapter Six: Creating New Neural Pathways 47

SECTION THREE: Your Personal Change Blueprint 55

Chapter Seven: Overview of the Eight-Step Personal Change Blueprint 57
- Step One – Your Payoffs and Your *Now* Statement 58
- Step Two – Identifying the Desired Outcome that Explains Exactly What You Want 61
- Step Three – Your Evidence Because You Have Accomplished this Outcome 63
- Step Four – Imagery Associated with the Accomplishment of this Outcome 65
- Step Five – Sounds Associated with the Accomplishment of this Outcome 66
- Step Six – Feelings Associated with the Accomplishment of this Outcome 67
- Step Seven – What Having this Accomplishment Does for You 67
- Step Eight – Influences on the Key Areas of Life 68

SECTION FOUR: Make It Yours 73

Chapter Eight: A Template and Some Examples . 75
- Example 1 – Self-Hypnosis for Procrastination 79
- Example 2 – Self-Hypnosis for Sleep 86
- Example 3 – Self-Hypnosis for Test Anxiety 93

- Example 4 – Self-Hypnosis for Public Speaking Anxiety 101
- Example 5 – Self-Hypnosis for Weight Loss 110
- Example 6 – Self-Hypnosis for Smoking ... 121

Conclusion 137
References 141

Introduction

Self-hypnosis is one of the most versatile and valuable tools you can have in your toolbox of self-help options. Why use self-hypnosis when you can go to a hypnotist for the same thing? Time and money. Self-hypnosis is free, and because we think 80% faster than we talk, you can develop a successful self-hypnosis practice and spend just ten minutes a day creating personal and permanent change in your life.

How does it work? It is all about rewiring your mind, except that instead of having wires in our brains, we have neural pathways. Let me start by explaining that everything we do, the good, the bad, and the ugly, is possible only because we have neural pathways in our brains that allow us to do everything we do. We can change a behavior by creating new neural pathways, whether we want to create a new habit or delete an old one.

You can hire me, or another professionally certified hypnotist, to help you make changes in your life, or you can learn to do it yourself using self-hypnosis. You can hire a psychologist to listen to you talk about all your problems over and over and figure out why you do the things you do, but you will most likely keep doing them. You can go to your doctor and get a prescription and see if medication helps you stop doing the things that you do not want to do anymore, or you can learn how to practice self-hypnosis.

I am not suggesting that self-hypnosis is a replacement for therapy and/or medication, nor am I suggesting you start or stop going to therapy or that you start or stop taking medication. Let me make that clear. I am not suggesting that self-hypnosis is a replacement for medication and/or therapy. I am not suggesting that by learning the methods in this book, you no longer need medication and/or therapy. I am suggesting that by learning the material in this book and fully understanding why you do the things you do, you will better understand how to change many of those unwanted beliefs and/or behaviors on your own using self-hypnosis.

How to Get the Most Out of this Book

I have organized this book into four sections. *Section One–Self Hypnosis is Easy* gives the basic framework of all you need to know to practice self-hypnosis. This section was originally designed to be the last section of the book. But, not everyone is interested in wading through chapter after chapter on how the brain works, how to use my eight-step process called your Personal Change Blueprint, or looking at examples of how to use the Personal Change Blueprint for procrastination, sleep, test anxiety, public speaking anxiety, weight loss, or smoking. So, I have written the last part first, just for you! Once you have read Chapter One – How to Practice Self-Hypnosis, you will have your curiosity satisfied about how to practice self-hypnosis, and you will have lots of questions that will be answered by reading the rest of the book. Brilliant, right?

Putting yourself or another person into the state of hypnosis is easy. The art and skill of the hypnotist come in knowing what to say to the subject or how to deliver suggestions to yourself via your thoughts in the case of self-hypnosis once the state of hypnosis is achieved. If you already know what to do once you are in the hypnotic state but are unsure how to get to that state, then section one will teach you everything you need to know about getting into the hypnotic state to carry out self-hypnosis.

However, if you are interested in learning more about how the conscious and subconscious parts of your mind work, why you do the things you do, and what you can do about it, you will get a lot of value from *Section Two – Neural Pathways and How the Subconscious Mind Works*. I encourage you to read through the entire book for a thorough understanding of self-hypnosis, how it works, and why it works.

I have been a certified hypnotist since 2008 and a certified hypnosis instructor since 2012. During my career, I have developed a process that I use with every client for every issue. This is an eight-step process called your Personal Change Blueprint. During a client session, as I am interviewing the client and filling out their unique blueprint, I tell them we are choreographing the concepts and words I will use for their maximum benefit during their hypnosis session.

I encourage you to read this section, *Section Three – Your Personal Change Blueprint*, to become familiar with the structure and the reasoning behind how I teach someone to create and use their own Personal Change Blueprint. The information you write down on your Personal Change Blueprint will be the words you say back to yourself while you are practicing self-hypnosis.

Like I said, getting yourself into the state of hypnosis is easy; we actually go in and out of hypnosis several times each day. It is a completely normal state. Knowing how to deliver suggestions in a way that makes positive change is where the art and skill of the hypnotist comes in. This is all shared in section three.

In *Section Four – Make It Yours,* I give several examples of common life issues that hypnosis can help. Examples help us further our understanding of any new skill. Here I have outlined how to fill out the Personal Change Blueprint with examples of some of the most common issues clients have. These issues include procrastination, sleep, test anxiety, public speaking anxiety, weight loss, and smoking. Remember, these examples show you only one possible way to fill out the Personal Change Blueprint. Multiple answers could go in each section, and there are no wrong answers. There *is* a right and wrong way to word the answers, however, and by the time you get to this section, you will be well versed in the how and why I express things the way I do when giving suggestions to my hypnosis clients.

I am excited to be teaching self-hypnosis in this format. For years, I have been teaching it in-person to clients and students in group settings and on Zoom. You can learn to practice self-hypnosis easily and effectively on your own using this process, or, if you prefer working with a pro, give me a call!

SECTION ONE

Self-Hypnosis is Easy

Chapter One

How to Practice Self-Hypnosis

What if you could wave a magic wand and be rid of all your bad habits? Can you see yourself waking up on time every morning feeling refreshed, wide awake, and rarin' to go? Can you imagine keeping all your stuff picked up and put away all the time just out of habit? Or maybe you would like to be that person who comes home from work at the end of the day full of energy and excitement to be home with your family! Maybe you want to quit smoking, slow down on the drinking, let your nails grow, enjoy public speaking, and learn to love yourself. You can do all this and more with self-hypnosis.

This is a book about you, why you do the things you do, and what you can do to either 1. *do them better* or 2. *stop doing them altogether.* This is a book about empowerment, liberating yourself from past programming, and creating the life you want for yourself. As mentioned in the introduction, I will start with the end in sight and give you the instructions on how to carry out self-hypnosis. After you have finished the first three chapters, you will know how to carry out self-hypnosis, but it will not be until you have completed the entire book that you will fully understand how to do it like a pro. Let's get started!

Creating the Right Environment

You can experience self-hypnosis in just about any environment as long as you can shut out external stimuli. You can even do it with your eyes open if you are really good! However, to get the best result, I recommend finding or creating an environment conducive to self-hypnosis, especially if you are just learning. In other words, some place where you can have some peace and quiet, some place where *no one* or *no-thing* will distract you.

To get the most out of your self-hypnosis practice, choose an environment that allows you to maintain a steady focus. That may be a quiet room with no music, no traffic sounds, and no evidence of life outside those four walls. However, you might do better in an environment buzzing with sound if you are like me. When I am in a quiet room with no outside stimuli, I am dreadfully distracted by any sound—my stomach growling, the house creaking, you name it.

When I was a student at the university, my favorite place to study was the cafeteria. There was too much noise, but none of it was specific. It was a buzz of sound, and I found it easy to concentrate without any one sound distracting me. On the other hand, studying in the library was impossible. It was too quiet! I was constantly distracted by the sound of someone scooting their chair, sniffing, or coughing. It was impossible for me to focus with so much noise.

Figure out what works best for you. Maybe you already have a perfect space to do your self-hypnosis, or maybe you will organize things to be just right each time you settle in for your self-hypnosis. If you have a meditation practice, you are already halfway there. Use the same setup for self-hypnosis that you use for meditation.

Plan Ahead

If you have a meditation practice, you may have noticed that it is common to have your body temperature drop a bit during meditation. The same is true for hypnosis. The meditative state and the hypnotic state are virtually the same. You may find it helpful to wear a sweater or have a throw blanket handy to keep you from being distracted when becoming chilly.

Be comfortable! The best position for self-hypnosis is the position you are comfortable with for about ten to fifteen minutes. Adjust accordingly if you get fidgety during any part of your self-hypnosis session. Moving around is not going to ruin your self-hypnosis session. I prefer sitting in a chair with a high enough back to support my head, and when relaxed and leaning back, my feet are flat on the floor. You can do that or recline and put your feet up.

During self-hypnosis, it is normal to drift in and out of sleep or awareness a bit. If you fall asleep, you may need to adjust the time of day you are practicing your self-hypnosis. You may also want to sit up a bit more, put your feet on the floor and turn the lights up a little brighter. Experiment with the best position for you.

Your Focus

Before you begin, you will want to have a plan in mind. What is it you are going to focus on? What new habit do you want to create? What part of your life will be better after you make some changes? If you are experienced with self-hypnosis, you already know how to deliver suggestions to yourself.

If you are just starting, keep reading. By the time you finish this book, you will completely understand how to get the most out of your hypnosis sessions. I recommend reading this entire book and then coming back to section one to review this section on how to do the self-hypnosis part of the hypnosis.

Hypnosis sessions are comprised of three different phases. The first part is where you settle in, do some breathing exercises, and get nice and relaxed. This is called the induction. I use progressive relaxation and then a deepener that consists of a countdown from ten to one. This will make more sense if you have listened to this hypnosis recording available on my website debbietaylor-author.com

Once you are nice and relaxed, you are ready for the middle phase of hypnosis. This is where you give yourself positive suggestions based on the information you wrote down on your Personal Change Blueprint. It is vitally important that you remember to use language that creates the imagery of what you *do* want. Mentally rehearse your suggestions a few times.

After you have mentally rehearsed suggestions from your Personal Change Blueprint or ideas you have come up with, you are ready for the final phase of the hypnosis session, where you gently emerge from the hypnotic state and enter back into your normal waking consciousness. The next chapter will give you the steps to follow to experience a self-hypnosis session.

Chapter Two

The Process

1. Find someplace where you can get comfortable and where you will not be disturbed. If you have a recliner, great! If not, sit on your bed against the headboard with your legs stretched out. Or, just sit in a comfy chair. I do not recommend laying down because you want to avoid going all the way to sleep. You may find it helpful to use an eye mask to keep the room nice and dark.

2. Begin the induction, the first of three phases of the hypnotic experience, by taking in a deep, deep breath. Hold that to the count of three, four, or five, and then gently release. Do this two more times, making each inhalation a little deeper than the one before. After the third exhalation, bring all your

focus up around the top of your head and begin to relax your scalp, forehead, and eyebrows. Think about all the little muscles around your eyes and mouth . . . notice how they begin to soften with relaxation as you release any tension or tightness anywhere in and around the face, the neck, the throat.

Follow that flow of relaxation down into the shoulders and let it cascade over the shoulders flowing gently through the arms, all the way to the hands, releasing any tension or tightness from the fingertips.

3. Now, bring your focus back to the larger muscle groups of the upper back and chest. Notice how those muscles begin to soften with relaxation as you feel the warmth of that relaxation beginning to melt down the spine. Follow that warmth as it moves into the shoulder blades, down into the rib cage . . . flowing all through the middle back . . . down into the lower back . . . through the pelvis . . . and into the thighs.

4. Feel the release of any tension or tightness through the thighs as if it were simply evaporating through the pores of your skin. Follow the flow of that release through the knees . . . into the calves . . . all along the shins . . . through the ankles . . . and into the feet, as

you release any tension or tightness right through the tips of your toes. You are doing beautifully.

5. There are two ways we relax—physically and mentally—and you have just completed the process for physical relaxation. For mental relaxation, I want you to count down from ten to one, visualizing yourself walking down ten steps into a beautiful garden, or perhaps you are in an elevator going down one floor after another after another. Or perhaps you are on the beach.

   As you look at the wet sand, you notice that with each number you count, you can see that number as if it were etched into the wet sand. As those waves gently roll in and dissolve the numbers right before your eyes, you feel yourself falling deeper and deeper into relaxation, deeper and deeper within yourself as those waves gently roll out. Count slowly, rhythmically, and feel yourself dropping deeper and deeper into relaxation, deeper and deeper within yourself with each breath you take.

6. Once you have reached this state, it is time to mentally rehearse the suggestions you want to give yourself or the information you wrote down in your eight-step Personal Change Blueprint. This is the middle phase of the self-hypnosis process. As you go over the information in your Personal Change Blueprint, it does not matter if you change the order

of the material in your blueprint. It does not matter if you forget a detail here and there; you will be doing this again the next day. You will think of information that would have been a great addition to your blueprint, so add it. Just think of it as a movie in your mind—your mind-movie! Remember to use language that creates the imagery of what you *do* want if you add something new. Review the information as if you were watching a mind-movie of your new life story. Review it a few times.

7. Once you have gone over the suggestions from your Personal Change Blueprint a few times, you are ready to bring yourself back into your environment, back into normal waking consciousness, phase three of the self-hypnosis process. This is an excellent time to review the main idea of your outcome one more time as you begin counting up from one to five.

   To return to the waking state of consciousness, take a deep breath with each number you count up to five. Beginning at one, start wiggling your fingers and toes to kick up your circulation a bit . . . two, feel the cushion beneath you . . . three, notice how good you feel . . . four, take in a deep, deep breath and gather all that beautiful energy as you . . . five, exhale and gently open your eyes. Look around your environment and give yourself a minute or so to acclimate back into the world.

Congratulations! You just completed a thirty-minute self-hypnosis experience in about ten minutes. The more often you practice self-hypnosis, the less time it takes to get into the trance state, and the quicker you can experience it each day.

Follow this process every single day. Make it a habit. Repetition creates new neural pathways in your brain and aligns the focus of your conscious mind with the focus of the subconscious mind. You will learn more about this in the next section.

In case you missed it, here is a free hypnosis recording for you to listen to. This will give you an idea of how I use the process you just read about. Grab your download here, or scan the QR code provided.

What It Looks Like When I Practice Self-Hypnosis

I experience self-hypnosis practically every day, first thing in the morning. I am a bit slow to wake up in the morning, so embracing self-hypnosis first thing is a perfect fit for me. I wake up, use the bathroom to avoid later being distracted by body urges, and then settle into a comfy place to sit with my feet flat on the floor. I have learned the hard way that if I go back to bed and try this, I fall asleep, even if I am sitting up.

I get settled in and start with some deep breathing. Because I have been doing this for so long, I am conditioned to go into the hypnotic state as soon as the deep breathing starts. I continue, allowing any tension or tightness to release with each exhalation. Once I am fully relaxed, I review whatever I want to work on and assess the value it has brought to my life up until this point. I confirm appreciation for the value and that I am ready to give that up now because it is no longer bringing value into my life. (Follow the structure that you will be learning about in *Section Three – Your Personal Change Blueprint*).

For example, at the time of this writing, I am focusing on my eating habits. Until recently, I have gone overboard with a freedom-to-eat-whatever mindset. As a result, a few extra pounds have found their way to my body.

The value this freedom-to-eat-whatever mindset has brought into my life can be described as instant gratification, soothing, and convenience. I admit I have resorted to my college days of ordering pizza delivery, consuming chips and beer for dinner, and eating ice cream straight from the carton. It has been delightful, and now it is not. My pants are tight, I look frumpy, and I feel like a chubby old lady.

The internal dialog about looking at the value of the unwanted habit and stating why it is no longer of value is step one of the Personal Change Blueprint process. It starts by acknowledging the value of instant gratification, the ease of having food delivered, and the unbridled joy of eating whatever I damn well please, whenever I please, and wherever I please. Next, allow me to firmly state that the value of the aforementioned behaviors is no longer adding value to my life; they are creating problems, and I am now ready for change. I state the change, and then I mentally rehearse all the wonderful things in my life that will happen because I have regained control of my eating habits. This structure will be explained in the first step of your Personal Change Blueprint (your payoffs and your now statement).

Here is an example of the phrases I use when I am stating my desired change and the shifts that will prove to me I have accomplished my goal:

I enjoy eating twice each day, at noon and at dinner time, and easily delete any thoughts or images of eating at any other time.

As I say this to myself, I envision . . .

. . . my finger hitting the delete button on my computer keyboard repeatedly as the screen in front of me goes blank anytime I start

thinking about junk food. When I imagine myself at the grocery store, and as I look into my shopping cart, I see lots of fresh organic fruits and vegetables and lean meats. I see myself tiny again, fitting into my size small jeans, feeling good about my appearance whether I am in the yard pulling weeds, out in public, or standing on a stage giving a presentation.

I see myself at a restaurant . . .

. . . remembering that the fun of being in the restaurant is being with a good friend or a loved one; it is not about the food. I see myself at an event or special occasion focused on why I am there, and it is not about the food. I find it easy and natural to enjoy small portions of healthy, nutritious foods in just the right amounts at just the right times in all situations.

It takes me longer to type all this than it does to mentally rehearse it in self-hypnosis. In self-hypnosis, I go over the main points a few times, and then I bring myself back to awareness and carry on with my day. It is just this easy, but consistency is the key!

CHAPTER THREE

Common Questions About "Doing" Self-Hypnosis

You likely have some questions about the self-hypnosis process, and I want to answer them for you. Having taught self-hypnosis for over two decades, the following questions are the most commonly asked ones.

Q1: What is the best time of day to do self-hypnosis, and can I do it more than once each day?

First, let me explain: You will not be *doing* self-hypnosis. You will *experience* self-hypnosis. Because we go through the brain wave state of theta as we wake up each morning, I typically recommend experiencing self-hypnosis first thing in the morning. However, if you wake up bright-eyed and bushy-tailed, and you hit the ground running, then the morning is perhaps not the best time for you to experience self-hypnosis. For you, I recommend the evening between dinner and bedtime but not necessarily *at* bedtime because you do not want to fall asleep in the middle. It is okay to drift in and out of what will feel like sleep.

If neither morning nor evening works for you, choose a time in the middle of the day when you can take a break, clear your mind, and find some place to be alone. You may find that mornings work best on the weekends, and evenings work best during the week. Experiment and find out what works best for you.

First thing in the morning is preferable because you are already so close to that theta brain state (explained in more detail later) that it is easy to get right back to it.

You can experience self-hypnosis intentionally as many times throughout the day as you want, but do not do this while driving. If you fall asleep when experiencing self-hypnosis, make yourself less comfortable. In other words, sit up straighter, put the lights on brighter, and put your feet on the floor.

Q2: Where should I do self-hypnosis?

It is easy to create the right environment to carry out self-hypnosis. You will need somewhere to recline or just lean back a bit. If you have a recliner, great; otherwise, adjust the pillows on your bed and perch yourself up. Turn the lights down low, take your shoes off, and put your feet up. Close your eyes or use an eye mask if you like. If you have pets, either let them onto your lap, to begin with, or put them someplace where they will not bother you. Use earbuds or headphones if you are piping in music or if you have made a recording of the suggestions that you created from your Personal Change Blueprint. It is common to drop a degree or two in temperature when meditating or practicing hypnosis, so put on a sweater or have a throw blanket handy.

Q3: How do I deliver the suggestions I have created or the information from my Personal Change Blueprint once I am in the hypnotic state?

You have several choices regarding the delivery of suggestions from your Personal Change Blueprint or the suggestions you have come up with on your own if you are not using the Personal Change Blueprint. With either of these options, coming up with your own suggestions or completing your Personal Change Blueprint, I encourage you to mentally review the information several times before you start. Memorize it if you need to.

If you are using the Personal Change Blueprint, which I highly recommend, you will notice a pattern to the questioning, making it easier to remember what comes next. My preference is for you to review the information before you experience self-hypnosis and then remember it by thinking of the story it is telling. It is okay to remember things in a different order than you wrote them. Just think of it as your story, your mind-movie—and you get to make it any way you want.

You can also make a hypnosis recording for yourself. It will take longer to listen to than if you mentally rehearsed the information, but that should not be a problem unless you are in a big hurry. We tend to think about 80% faster than we speak, so listening to a recording will take more time. You could also have someone you know make the recording for you, especially if you do not like the sound of your own voice.

Another option is to summarize your suggestions or your Personal Change Blueprint information and write them on an index card. After you have finished the induction, simply give yourself the suggestion that in a moment, you are going to open your eyes to go over the suggestions from your Personal Change Blueprint. You will stay in a nice deep state of relaxation during the review. Then open your eyes, review the suggestions you have written down a few times, close your eyes, and emerge yourself from the hypnotic state to full conscious awareness.

If you have ever seen a stage hypnosis show, you will likely recall the volunteers on stage have their eyes open and are very active, but they are still in hypnosis. Opening your eyes in hypnosis does not necessarily take you out of hypnosis.

Q4: How many days should I stay on the same subject?

Repetition is the name of the game when it comes to rewiring your brain and creating new neural pathways, also known as habits. I recommend staying on one subject for ten days to two weeks before exploring the next subject. You will most likely start to notice changes much sooner than that and may be tempted to move on to the next subject right away. Do not do it! It is important to reinforce the suggestions from your Personal Change Blueprint over and over. It is like practicing a new song on a musical instrument. You have to practice the song several times to get good at it. Just because you get it right once does not mean you can stop practicing; you want the song embedded fully. Similarly, you want the suggestions from your Personal Change Blueprint to be deeply embedded in your subconscious mind so that your conscious mind and subconscious mind become congruent.

Q5: What if I miss a day?

No problem, get back to it the next day. If you are practicing self-hypnosis in the mornings and you forget one morning or just do not have time, go ahead and do it later in the day or the evening. Remember, the beauty of self-hypnosis is that you can complete an entire session in ten minutes or less. The more often you do it, the sooner you will align your conscious and subconscious mind, and the quicker you will see the proof that you are making the changes you set out to make.

That is it for instructions on how to practice self-hypnosis. Easy, isn't it? The most important part of the self-hypnosis experience is the giving of suggestions. There *is* a right way and a wrong way to do this. If you word your suggestions the wrong way, you could easily be reinforcing the very behavior you are trying to extinguish. Continue reading for more understanding of how and why it matters to word your suggestions correctly.

SECTION TWO

Neural Pathways and How the Subconscious Mind Works

Chapter Four

It Is All About Neural Pathways

Everything we do as humans is possible because we have a brain full of neural pathways. The way you pick up a fork (the fact that you *can* pick up a fork), the way you blink your eyes, turn a doorknob, drive a car, or scratch an itch, is only possible because you have corresponding neural pathways in your brain that are patterned to allow you to do what you do.

Think about this. When you were born, you did not have the neural pathways in your brain allowing you to tie your shoes. At about the age of four or five, someone showed you how to tie your shoes, and you were very motivated to learn how. You wanted to be a *big kid* and get the well-deserved pat on the head because you learned how to tie your shoes. This motivation, also known as a heightened emotional state, is key in forming new habits. So, you practiced over and over and over. Repetition is also key in forming new habits, and by habits, I mean neural pathways. That is what habits are; they are neural pathways in your brain. When people talk about rewiring the brain, they are talking about restructuring neural pathways.

As you practiced tying your shoes repeatedly, your brain started making a new set of neural pathways representing this new behavior. Once your brain figured out that you were doing it the same way repeatedly, it knew the new behavior was complete, finalized, and nothing new was being added, so it packaged it up, so to speak, and put it in the archives. Every time you need to tie your shoes, that specific grouping of neural pathways is awakened or activated, and—Boom!—you tie your shoes. When you are done, the pattern of neural pathways goes back into the archives. If you could compare the way you tie your shoes today with how you learned to tie them when you were a kid, you would see that you do it exactly the same now as you did then.

If something happened to you, an accident or an illness, and these specific neural pathways were injured or severed, you would not for the life of you remember how to tie your shoes. You can tie your shoes because you have specific neural pathways in your brain. Neural pathways got created through repetition and reinforced by a heightened state of emotion when you were a little kid. Isn't that crazy? Every single thing you do is because you have a head full of neural pathways. It makes wearing that bike helmet a little more important, doesn't it?

Would you like to see this in action? I have a really interesting video showing actual neural pathways being created. If you would like to see neural pathways in action, you can go to my website at **debbietaylor-author.com** or scan the QR code provided for access to the video. I love showing this to my clients and students. It is quite interesting to see what it looks like inside your brain when you are learning something new.

A great metaphor that helps to envision neural pathways and their creation is to think of a big green meadow of grass and the idea that you want to make a well-worn path from one edge of the meadow to another. This is a metaphor for creating a new habit. If you wanted to make a dirt trail in this meadow of grass, you could walk across the grass several times in the same place and then take a look at where you have been. If you did this, you would be able to see where you walked back and forth, but if you stop after just a few passes, the grass will bounce back, and there will be no evidence of what you started. If you want a really dominant well-worn path, meaning a well-established new habit, you would need to go back and forth in the same place along that path until there was a well-established dirt trail.

Making a dirt trail like this is similar to the idea of making new neural pathways, or in this case, a new habit. New neural pathways are created by repetition or trauma. I make hypnosis recordings for all my clients and instruct them to listen to their recordings daily for about two weeks. This repetition creates new neural pathways, also known as the new habit they are after. For this reason, I recommend that you choose a topic to focus on and stick with it for ten days to two weeks before moving on to the next idea.

I mentioned that trauma also creates neural pathways. In terms of your meadow of green grass, experiencing trauma is like having a back-hoe plow through your beautiful meadow of green grass and leaving a giant path right through the middle of it. This giant path is a well-established neural pathway of trauma. Unfortunately, trauma often gets reinforced with repetition because the trauma victim has to explain what happened to the police, the insurance company, their doctors, friends, family, and people at work, and then they think about it repeatedly, which all serves to continually re-traumatize them. You will learn in a later section that the subconscious mind does not actually have to be doing something to create or reinforce neural pathways. It can just be thinking about doing it and get almost the same result.

Trauma does not always have to be a huge, monumental event. Usually, when we think of trauma, we think of a horrific car accident or something major, but a minor fender bender can have just as much of a devastating effect on the driver as a horrific accident.

I worked with a woman once who was so depressed and upset with her mother because, in the client's reality, her mother had ruined her wedding day. She was incredibly upset about her mother's behavior and couldn't stop obsessing over it. Her obsession was creating problems for her at work. She could not sleep and was very, very depressed over it.

In my imagination, I envisioned her mother at the wedding dancing naked on the tables, drunk, making a spectacle of herself, or worse. When I asked her to tell me what her mother had done, I was surprised to learn that, while her mother didn't dance naked on the tables, the upsetting behavior she did carry out had actually occurred *after* the wedding.

It was about two weeks after the wedding. My client had gotten all the wedding pictures back from the photographer and was excitedly looking at them with her mother. Her mother hated the way she (the mother) looked in every picture and complained about her appearance in every photo.

This was the basis for the emotional trauma my client was experiencing. Her mother's negative comments about the way she looked in the wedding photos *ruined the whole wedding* in my client's mind. Every time she relived the experience of looking at the wedding pictures with her mom, she got more upset.

She complained about it to her husband, sisters, friends, and pretty much anyone who would listen. She was emotionally traumatized and blamed her mother for ruining the entire wedding.

Over reaction? Maybe for you or me, but it was not for her. It was significant for her, and she was retraumatizing herself every time she relived it, either through her thoughts or words. Repetition can work for us or against us. She practiced being the victim in this situation every day, and she got good at it.

What kinds of things can you think about that you have gotten better at because of repetition? Was it learning a new song on the guitar or piano? How about practicing your drawing or painting skills? Was it a sport? Why do coaches put their athletes through drills, doing the same things repeatedly? They may or may not know about neural pathways, but they know how repetition creates new habits and new skills.

What kinds of things did you get better at that you wish you had not? Smoking, driving recklessly, looking in the mirror, berating yourself, complaining, watching the news, or perhaps snacking on junk food every time you watch television?

Any behavior we want to change can be changed through repetition, but we have to practice it the way we *want* it to be. This is why I suggest that once you choose an idea to focus on during self-hypnosis, you stick with it for ten days to two weeks. You will start noticing change sooner than that and will be tempted to think you are ready to move on. Remember seeing the grass lying down in the meadow after just a few repetitions? Staying on the same self-hypnosis subject for just a few days is not enough. Keep up with the same suggestions for ten days to two weeks, and you will have created new neural pathways in your brain that are permanent, hard-wired, and translate into the new behaviors you want for yourself.

Chapter Five

Where Do Neural Pathways Come From?

Before we launch into a conversation about the conscious and subconscious mind, let's talk more about neural pathways and where they come from.

There are three main sources of neural pathways.

First, we are born with lots of them! It is kind of like new computers that come loaded with programs already installed. As infants, our bodies function as well as they do only because our neural pathways have developed according to plan. Because of our neural pathways, our little bodies have functioning digestive systems, immune systems, circulatory systems, and so forth. Our eyes can blink, and our throats can swallow.

Doctors know how to test all these systems to ensure everything has developed correctly. If you have ever taken a newborn in for a checkup, you may remember the doctor testing the baby's reflexes by running a finger or an instrument along the bottom of the baby's foot. They are checking to make sure the baby's reflexes, and many other things, are working right and that all systems are go. If they are not working properly, it is due to a glitch in the development of the neural pathways connected to that part of the body.

The second source of neural pathway acquisition is life experience. As we live our lives, we learn and grow and expand our capacity for neural pathways at every moment of every day. Most of this growing and learning is unconscious. You could say we acquire neural pathways by default, by the mere fact that we exist. This is especially true for us as little kids. We are a bit like the video recorders on our phones, we observe and absorb everything in our experience, and through the repetition of experience, more neural pathways are created. I have more to say about this in the section on brain waves.

A third way neural pathways are acquired is through intention. As humans, we have the ability to exercise volition. This means we can decide to do something and then act on that decision. This is what hypnosis is all about—the intentional creation of new neural pathways, also known as habits, rituals, routines, beliefs, values, and so on, through repetition combined with an elevated emotional state.

Conscious Mind and Subconscious Mind

You are learning more about yourself and why you do the things you do. Let's add a better understanding of the conscious mind and the subconscious mind and what brain waves have to do with hypnosis. As adults, we have conscious and subconscious parts of our mind at work. Lucky for us, they work in tandem.

The conscious part of your mind is the part of your mind that hears me when I am talking to you. You are awake, alert, alive, and you know where you are and what you are doing. Your conscious mind is the part of your mind capable of analyzing, comparing, and contrasting; it is where your volition is. When you make up your mind to do something, that decision is conscious. Most of us feel like we are aware of and in control of our decisions every day.

The subconscious part of your mind is the habit mind. When your brain accesses the neural pathways connected to tying your shoes, playing the piano, and everything else, your subconscious mind is doing this. The subconscious part of your mind is where you house your habits, rituals, routines, beliefs, values, memories, and so on. All the systems in our bodies that have been working since conception are happening at the subconscious level. The majority of what is going on with us, as humans, is happening at the subconscious level.

The conscious part of your mind is processing information at 40 bits of data/second. Compare this to the subconscious mind processing information at 40 million bits of data/second. Another way of looking at this is to say that we are only aware of and in conscious control of 1-5% of what is going on during any given time. That means the subconscious part of the mind is running the show the remaining 95-99% of that time. I know this is hard to grasp, but realize that we are not aware of all that is going on in the subconscious mind because it is below the level of conscious awareness, hence the name subconscious.

The Critical Faculty

An invisible wall stands between the conscious mind and the subconscious mind, referred to as the critical faculty or the critical factor. This critical factor makes it difficult for us to make changes easily. This wall is the obstacle keeping you from engaging in the new behaviors you want to adopt for weight loss, quitting smoking, sleeping better, studying more often, stopping procrastinating, and so on.

My weight loss clients get so frustrated because they *know* how to put a healthy meal together; they *know* what they should and should not be doing. They are not stupid.

Clients who want to quit smoking *know* that smoking is expensive, smelly, disgusting, and is killing them. They are not stupid. People with insomnia KNOW they need to stop worrying about everything under the sun and just go to sleep and stop complaining about it, yet they cannot. Do any of these examples describe you? It is hard to do the things we know we should be doing because this knowingness comes from the *conscious* part of the mind, a measly 1-5% of the equation.

The momentum of the subconscious mind can be pretty overpowering. Luckily, self-hypnosis can reprogram that momentum to work in our favor. Hypnosis is how we get the subconscious mind to *know* the same thing the conscious mind has known all along.

Hopefully, you are beginning to understand that even on your best day, fully motivated and ready for change, your conscious mind only contributes 1-5% of what is needed to make a new habit change. The conscious mind is up against the enormous momentum of the subconscious mind.

Keep in mind the programs of the subconscious mind are completely impersonal. There is no part of *you* in the subconscious mind that is monitoring what is going on. No part of *you* in the subconscious mind is saying what is good or bad, helpful, or unhelpful. It really is a lot like a computer program, and the neural pathways in your brain are as impersonal as the programs in your computer.

So what can we do about it? How can we bust through that wall, the critical faculty, speak directly to the subconscious mind, and make the changes we want to improve our life experiences? Take a guess.

For some people, this wall, the critical faculty, is a thin veil. Some people are highly sensitive and highly suggestable. This is not to be confused with being gullible, and it has nothing to do with that. Being highly sensitive can be difficult if you do not understand how to filter out incoming data. Many of the clients I work with that are highly sensitive are people with phobias. The good news is that highly sensitive people are usually excellent hypnosis subjects because they are so receptive to suggestions. I jokingly say, "I love a good phobia," only because clients with phobias typically respond beautifully to hypnosis.

On the other hand, many people's critical faculty is not quite so thin. Sometimes, but not always, these people tend to be more analytical and very linear in their thinking. When I am working with clients, part of my job is to get a feel for their degree of analytical thinking skills relative to their visualization skills. Knowing this helps me choose just the proper technique for them.

When doing self-hypnosis, if you tend to be highly analytical, you may notice that it takes you a little longer to get into that hypnotic state than you had planned. Do not let that deter you. Keep at it and it will not take long until your brain is wired to go *into* the state of hypnosis. Then every time you experience self-hypnosis, you will get to that state quicker and quicker.

Understanding the nuances between the conscious mind, the subconscious mind, and the critical faculty makes it easier to understand how and why hypnosis is such a great process for making change at the subconscious level.

Are you ready for the secret to getting through the critical faculty? You are likely expecting something profound, something magical and mystical.

I hate to disappoint you, but it is all about relaxation. That is it, relaxation. Why? When we relax, I mean really relax, physically and mentally, our brain waves slow down. We are still aware of what is going on; we do not go off into magic land. We just feel really good. When our brain waves slow down and go into the theta state, that invisible wall, the critical faculty, becomes very permeable.

This allows us to take what the conscious mind wants and present it to the subconscious mind without any resistance. There is a right and a wrong way to do this, more about this coming up, but suffice it to say that by getting yourself into a nice state of relaxation in self-hypnosis, you create the opportunity for your conscious mind to be in direct communication with your subconscious mind.

As you repeat this communication correctly, you create new neural pathways that reflect the desired behavior. You naturally find yourself living with new eating habits, new sleeping habits, new study habits, and more.

Hypnosis is not the only way to make change. Let me be perfectly clear about that. There are plenty of examples of people who have accomplished great feats without the use of hypnosis, not consciously anyway. Hypnosis just happens to make a lot of sense to me, and I am passionate about teaching people how their mind works and how hypnosis, done correctly, can improve one's quality of life. Self-hypnosis can be done anytime, at any place, and for any reason.

There are many different approaches and techniques to use when it comes to doing self-hypnosis. The good news is that almost all of them work. The process I am teaching you here is my process. This is the process I use for myself and have used with clients and students since 2008. I tell you this to avoid any confusion you may have after watching YouTube videos with hypnotists demonstrating stage hypnosis or rapid inductions.

Everyone is different. Try the process I am teaching you here, and then explore other options if you are curious. Find what works for you!

Now you know that relaxation can slow your brain waves to theta, which results in clear communication between your conscious mind and your subconscious mind. I want to share more about brainwave states and how they relate to hypnosis.

Brainwave States

There are four stages of brain wave activity we will look at. From slowest to fastest, they are delta, theta, alpha, and beta. As adults, we experience each of these brainwave states throughout the day, depending on where we are and what is going on around us.

Delta is the slowest of the brainwave states. As adults, if we are in delta, we are in a very deep, dreamless sleep or in a coma. As infants, we are in the delta state for about the first two years of our lives (Laibow, R., 1999). Clearly, infants are not in comas, but they do not *interact* with their environment like we do as adults. Their little brains are like video recorders. They observe and absorb everything in their environment. As they do so, they are creating millions of neural pathways based on what they are experiencing—the good, the bad, and the ugly.

They do not yet have the cognitive ability to compare, contrast, or analyze what they are experiencing. They do not even have language skills yet, so they are not processing in terms of words. You know when you get older, and you recognize your parents in your behavior? This is where it comes from. Everything you experienced as an infant is recorded in your brain in the form of neural pathways and becomes the *norm* according to your subconscious mind.

Next up is **Theta.** As children, we evolve from the delta state to the theta state at around age two and have access to delta and theta exclusively until we are around six or seven. Theta is my favorite because this is the brainwave state most often associated with hypnosis. Depending on what you read or who the author is, sometimes the alpha/theta state is considered more closely related to hypnosis. You can get into this state that allows clear and open communication between your conscious mind and your subconscious mind as you practice self-hypnosis. And you will recall, you get into this state through relaxation.

Theta state is fun! This is where we combine reality and fantasy; not yet having the ability to discern between the two, it is easy to understand why kids at this age easily believe in Santa Claus, the Easter Bunny, the Tooth Fairy, and so on. Again, children at this age are not interacting with their environment the way we do as adults. They are recording, observing, and absorbing everything in their environment free from the filters of analyzing, comparing, and contrasting.

As adults, we go into this theta state at least twice each day and sometimes more. We always go through the theta state, right as we wake up in the morning and right as we fall asleep at night. This is why I recommend doing self-hypnosis first thing in the morning. You are already so close to that theta state that it is easy to get right back to it.

Around the ages of six or seven, our brains evolve into the **Alpha** state. This is a big deal because, for the first time, we have the ability to analyze, compare, and contrast. This is the birth of the *conscious* mind. Up until this point, we have been operating only from the subconscious mind, in a state of hypnosis, you could say.

All of a sudden, the idea of a jolly fat man in a red suit flying around the world in a sleigh, delivering presents to everyone in one night, is preposterous. Before our brains evolved into the alpha state, it made perfect sense. All the programs and neural pathways created from birth to this point remain active and unchanged until you consciously access this vast warehouse of the subconscious mind and update your programs. What beliefs and values did you acquire as a child are in direct opposition to what you believe now as an adult?

Once we evolve into the alpha state, we are able to process information in a more sophisticated manner. We can do higher-level math problems, we are more socially aware, and the world takes on a very different quality than in previous stages of development.

Our brain development takes another leap into maturity around the age of twelve as we enter the **Beta** brain wave state. Over time the beta brain wave state continues to refine its development into low, middle, and high beta brain wave activity. This is where we spend much of our time as adults as we manage our hectic and sometimes chaotic life schedules.

Understanding the role brainwaves play in self-hypnosis is important. Relaxation creates the ideal environment for personal change by helping you access the ideal brainwave state for self-hypnosis. This eliminates the barrier, the critical faculty, that keeps the subconscious mind from acting on or responding to the wishes of the conscious mind.

You may recall a popular children's story by Laura Numeroff and Felicia Bond, *If You Give a Mouse a Cookie*. This is a circular tale where one thing leads to another and then another, and so on. Explaining and understanding hypnosis is similar.

Start with getting comfortable. Take a few deep breaths and guide yourself into a state of relaxation following the process outlined in the first chapter. When you are in this relaxed state, your brainwaves slow down. Because your brainwaves have slowed down, you have two-way communication between the conscious and subconscious minds.

Now that you have two-way communication between the conscious and subconscious parts of your mind, your subconscious mind will review and "listen to" the prepared suggestions from the Personal Change Blueprint. As your subconscious mind reviews and listens to the language in your Personal Change Blueprint, it creates imagery (your mind movie) based on the words in the suggestions. By repeatedly reviewing your Personal Change Blueprint, your brain physically creates new neural pathways, creating the desired habit, behavior, and/or belief.

CHAPTER SIX

Creating New Neural Pathways

I have mentioned a few times that there is a right and wrong way to experience self-hypnosis. This has to do with the way you word the suggestions you give to yourself. The following section will clarify how to deliver suggestions the *right* way.

Important Fact #1: The subconscious mind, like a computer, speaks its own language, and it is the language of imagery. Everything you think about, talk about, or listen to is translated by your subconscious mind into imagery. This imagery is the content of all your programmed behaviors. Keep this in mind as I fine-tune this idea by explaining that your subconscious mind cannot construct a picture of you *not* doing something. I know that is a weird sentence. Let me explain and demonstrate.

In a moment, I am going to tell you *not* to do something. Get ready, prepare yourself *not* to do this thing I am going to tell you *not* to do. Are you ready? Here goes. Do *not*, under any circumstances, I repeat, do *not* . . . think of a red truck.

You thought of a red truck, didn't you? I know you did. You cannot help but think of a red truck even though I told you *not* to. It is just the way the mind works. The subconscious mind throws out words like *don't*, *won't*, *stop*, *quit,* and so on and creates the image of the rest of the sentence. Think about your internal dialog and what kind of imagery you are programming yourself with day in and day out. If you are like most people, the majority of your thoughts are about things you *do not* want to keep happening.

The more you think about what you do not want, the better you are at reinforcing the neural pathways related to what you do not want. You might be really good at worrying, really good at being angry, or really good at feeling like the victim. There is hypnosis for that!

When clients come to me and say they want to stop smoking, I know what they mean. I am not a computer, but when they say to *themselves* that they want to stop smoking, their subconscious mind just makes an image of them smoking.

Think of the image your subconscious mind creates when you repeat to yourself, *I will stop yelling at my kids. I will stop yelling at my kids. I will stop yelling at my kids!* Yes, you have made an image of yourself yelling at your kids. One of the most important skills to develop when carrying out self-hypnosis is to make sure you are thinking about your desired suggestions using words that create the image of what you *do* want to have happen.

If you say to yourself, *I want to stop smoking cigarettes after dinner every night*, what image did you just practice? If you say to yourself, *I want to stop tossing and turning all night*, what image did you just create? If you say to yourself, *I have got to stop worrying about my job all the time*, what did you just program yourself to do? This is a really important concept and will become more important as you combine this with the next very important thing to know about creating neural pathways.

Important Fact #2: The subconscious mind does not differentiate between having an actual experience or just thinking about having the experience. This is huge. This fact can work for us or against us, and we have the power to direct it to work *for* us if we know how. Let's take a deeper look at this idea.

Imagine sitting on your back patio on a lovely summer day, sunny, warm, and quiet, and you feel so happy. You are reading your favorite book, and all is well. And then, out of the corner of your eye, you notice something moving. You take a look, and—Yikes!—it is a giant spider, and it is on the patio running straight toward you.

Ack!!! Panic ensues! You scream bloody murder, and you jump out of your chair and run hysterically to the house. Your heart is beating out of your chest, and all you can think of is running for your life before that giant spider wrestles you to the ground and kills you. I understand some of you would not react this way but work with me here.

Fast forward, it is days later, and you are sitting in your living room watching television, perfectly relaxed. You are watching a show on nature, and all of a sudden—Bam!—there it is, an image of a giant spider! Your conscious mind knows it is just an image, but your heart is racing. You are transported to almost the same state you were in the other day on the patio. Your conscious mind knows it is just an image on the screen, but remember, your conscious mind is only contributing 1-5% of the knowledge of what is going on at any given time. Your subconscious mind is acting as if the event were happening all over again regardless of what your conscious mind knows to be true.

Or how about this, your friend comes over with a new puppy. This puppy is the cutest thing you have seen in ages! You get to hold it and snuggle it and kiss and hug it. The puppy is soft and fluffy and wiggly and warm. You love feeling the puppy in your hands and smelling that puppy breath, and your system is flooded with feel-good chemicals. You love the experience of being with that puppy.

Later on that day, you daydream about holding the puppy. You remember how much you loved holding it and how soft, fluffy, and warm it was. You remember that puppy breath and how cute it was. Once again, you are flooded with feel-good chemicals, only the puppy is nowhere to be seen. Get it? Your subconscious mind does not differentiate between having an experience and thinking about having the experience. This includes thinking about it, talking about it, listening to it, worrying about, or wishing for it.

The implications of these two important facts cannot be understated. You create your state of mind based on your brain's thoughts, even if it is thinking about something that happened in the past or something that has never happened at all. By repeating these thoughts, real or imagined, you either reinforce neural pathways that are already created or create new ones. In other words, you get really good at whatever you are focused on, whether you want it or not.

You have a good understanding of neural pathways, how we acquire them and how we can intentionally acquire them. You have learned the vital importance of structuring the suggestions you use in self-hypnosis the right way, meaning you understand that you must use language that creates the images of what you *do* want. And you can see that by pretending that what you want to occur has occurred, your subconscious mind will respond as if it were true in the here and now.

Let me put this together for you. Hypnosis is getting into a state of relaxation. When you are in a state of relaxation, your brain waves slow down. When your brain waves slow down, that wall (critical factor) between the conscious and subconscious mind dissolves. Now your subconscious mind is receptive and available to suggestions. As you mentally rehearse the suggestions of what you want to have happen, using words that create the imagery of what you want, you begin the process of creating new neural pathways. Through repetition of these carefully worded suggestions, these neural pathways become hard-wired, meaning they become permanent habits and/or beliefs. This can all be accomplished by doing self-hypnosis for eight to ten minutes each day. Are you ready to create suggestions that will result in fabulous transformation?

In the next section, my eight-step Personal Change Blueprint will be outlined to add more depth to the practice of self-hypnosis so that the suggestions you create result in absolute success. Once you are familiar with the process, it is easy to use it during every session of self-hypnosis. Having a daily practice of self-hypnosis has created beautiful changes in all areas of my life, including health, wealth, relationships, self-esteem, and spirituality, and I know it will do the same for you.

SECTION THREE

Your Personal Change Blueprint

Chapter Seven

Overview of the Eight-Step Personal Change Blueprint

Before I turn you loose to create your Personal Change Blueprint, I want to outline each step ahead of time to help put this into perspective. To get the most out of your self-hypnosis session, you need to settle on a topic to focus on. What area of your life needs a little updating? Is it your eating habits, relationships, or the way you conduct yourself at work or at home? Maybe you want to change your sleep habits? Choose something fun and easy at first so you can focus on learning how to do this in the best way possible. Once you have the process down, you can focus on the more pressing issues.

After I teach you about the eight-step Personal Change Blueprint process, I will share examples with you in the next section. There is also a template for you to copy as you create your own Personal Change Blueprint. Looking at examples of how other people have answered the eight-step Personal Change Blueprint questions will make it easier for you to understand how to create your own blueprint.

The information you put on your Personal Change Blueprint is the information you will mentally rehearse when you practice self-hypnosis. If you happen to choose the same topic as any of the examples, that does not mean those answers should be *your* answers. Personalize your answers. We could all choose the same topic to focus on, but our blueprints would all be different. Are you ready for a life-changing process to help you with your self-hypnosis practice? Here it is, your eight-step Personal Change Blueprint.

Step One – Your Payoffs and Your *Now* Statement

There is a belief that behind every behavior, there is a positive intention. I agree with this statement, but it deserves some explanation. Another way to look at this is to say that the subconscious mind always thinks it is doing something to help you even when some of the habits and behaviors we engage in are bad for us or hurt us. This is the positive intention. Your assignment is to figure out what kind of help it could be pointing at. To do this, sometimes, we have to look back to when a specific behavior was created to see what the positive intention was when the behavior became a habit.

For example, I started smoking cigarettes at a young age. By the time I was an adult and was ready to quit, there was no positive intention for the smoking habit, none at all. But, at the time the smoking habit was established, it was full of positive intentions. It was fun! I loved hanging out with the older kids. It made me feel part of something.

The act of smoking was emotionally connected to listening to great music on really good speakers, being at parties, associating with kids I liked and that liked me, free alcohol, and cute boys with long hair. I was accepted into this peer group, and I liked being a rebel. By the time I hit my thirties, however, there was no longer any positive intention, only the original payoff—the positive emotions—created when the habit was established.

Remember the neural pathways created when you learned to tie your shoes? Recall that once your brain figured out that you were tying them the same way every time, that nothing new was happening, those shoe-tying neural pathways got archived only to be awakened when you needed to tie your shoes. The same thing happens with smoking. Once my subconscious recognized that the behaviors involved in creating the neural pathways for smoking were the same every time, that habit got archived, with all the positive emotions I was experiencing *at that time*, as part of the habit.

Here in step one, you will be asked to identify the positive intentions or payoffs related to the unwanted habit and/or belief you want to change. These will be positive intentions that were or could have been relevant when the unwanted habit or belief was established.

These are the subconscious payoffs for engaging in that undesirable behavior. Remember, once a behavior is established and firmly rooted in your subconscious mind, it is boxed up and archived. The behavior is stored away and only brought out when you need it. These neural pathways and programs do not keep pace with your personal growth and development. These payoffs can be, and usually are, decades old.

Once you have identified one or more possible payoffs for that unwanted behavior, you are ready to let your subconscious mind know that you appreciate that positive intention but that you are prepared to thank it, bless it, and send it on its way.

Next, you will create your "***now***" statement. This is where you tell your subconscious mind that the past is over, things are changing regarding this behavior, and *now* this is how it will be. You are explaining to your subconscious mind why you are willing to give up those old positive intentions—the payoff.

Perhaps you gained a lot of weight when you went through a divorce. The payoff from that habit was the *comfort* of eating yummy foods that took your mind off your troubles for a few minutes. Your subconscious mind recognized the heightened state of positive emotion while you were engaged in that behavior and acted as though you were still getting that same value.

You can acknowledge your awareness of that payoff to your subconscious mind. You can let it know that you appreciate its attempts at helping you. You can acknowledge that *it was helpful at that time, but now, you are ready to reclaim your health* and be free from the need to comfort yourself with food. The examples in Section Four will help clarify this process and explain how others have answered this question.

Step Two – Identifying the Desired Outcome that Explains Exactly What You Want

If you were writing a story about creating this big change in your life, this step could be the title of your story—the main idea. Here you are identifying in a simple statement exactly what you want—not the *result* of having what you want, but what you *actually* want. This is an outcome statement. Many people think they want to lose weight but what they really want is to have a healthy relationship with food. Weight loss is the result of having what they want.

Sometimes this is hard to say in a way that describes what we want instead of what we do not want. My weight loss clients will tell me they do not want to obsess over food anymore. So I ask them what they will be doing if they are not obsessing over food anymore? Sometimes they will tell me they do not want to snack on junk food after dinner every night. So I ask them, what will you be doing if you are not snacking on junk food after dinner every night?

It is usually at this point they say they do not know what they would be doing because they had not thought about it. How can you change a behavior if you have not even thought about what you want to do instead? If you find yourself describing what you *do not* want as you work through your Personal Change Blueprint, just ask yourself, *If I am not doing [fill in the blank], what am I doing?* The Personal Change Blueprint is designed to get you thinking about and identifying what you want at a deeper level and in greater detail than you ever have before.

Once you get to Section Four of this book, you will see the examples I have provided to help you fill out your Personal Change Blueprint. The examples cover procrastination, sleep, test anxiety, public speaking anxiety, weight loss, or smoking. These examples will help you get a feel for creating your own Personal Change Blueprint. Your answers will be specific to you and your topic. Remember, your outcome statement must be a statement of what you *do* want rather than what you do not want.

Step Three – Your Evidence Because You Have Accomplished this Outcome

Once you reach this step, you will be filling it out (and the remaining steps) *as if* you have already accomplished your outcome—meaning you <u>*have accomplished*</u> your goal and the new habit and/or belief is just the new norm. This is important. Here you get to practice your pretending skills to the max.

I suggest that as you work your way through your Personal Change Blueprint, each time you start a new step, go back to step two and re-read your outcome, then re-read the information you put down for the next step so that you reinforce the new information and build on it. This will help bolster the impact of Your Personal Change Blueprint. Make sure you answer each question from the perspective of having already accomplished the outcome.

Read it back to yourself in a way that sounds like this,

Because I have manifested [fill in the blank with your desired outcome], I notice [the evidence].

Or,

When I think about having this change in my life, I see [the evidence].

Here in step three, you will be identifying the evidence proving and demonstrating to you that you have, in fact, accomplished your outcome. What changes do you notice, and what is different? If you find yourself saying things like, *I will have more energy*, or *I will be more productive*, flesh that out a little more. What kinds of things will you be doing with that energy? What will you be accomplishing because you are more productive?

As you develop your Personal Change Blueprint, you will be creating a magnificent mind movie to review in self-hypnosis. Make it rich, colorful, and full of detail. The sky is the limit!

Let me clarify this a bit more.

At **step three**, before you answer, go back to step two and re-read it to yourself as if you are telling a story in the present. Then add the details for step three.

At **step four**, before you answer, go back and re-read step two and step three. Then add the details for step four.

At **step five**, before you answer it, go back to step two, re-read it, then re-read step three and step four. Then <u>add the details for step five</u>.

At **step six**, before you answer, go back to and re-read step two, step three, step four, and step five. Then <u>add the details for step six</u>.

This is cumulative storytelling. As you go back and review the story from the beginning, you add more details, and your subconscious mind creates a mind-movie. The neural pathways are already beginning to form, and new ideas are being stimulated. This is where the real value of this process is happening. This is self-hypnosis on steroids!

Once you get to step seven, you do not need to review the previous steps, although it will not hurt anything if you do.

Step Four – Imagery Associated with the Accomplishment of this Outcome

In step four, you are asked to identify any *images* that come to mind when you think of having accomplished your outcome. It is okay if you repeat some of the information from one step to another. As you approach this part of your Personal Change Blueprint, you will ask yourself, *When I think of all the changes happening in my life because I have accomplished my outcome, I see [finish the thought]*.

Your answers may be literal or figurative. If you see yourself on the hillside dancing in the sunlight, then so be it. The more time you spend focusing on the results of having accomplished what you want, the more you stimulate ideas and images at the subconscious level. The more time you spend focusing on the results of accomplishing the outcome you want, the better you align the focus and desires of your conscious and subconscious minds.

Step Five – Sounds Associated with the Accomplishment of this Outcome

Have you ever thought about the changing sounds in your environment once you have created something new in your life? If you are focused on learning to play an instrument or becoming a singer, then the answer is probably yes. However, most of us do not pay much attention to sounds when we think about making changes in our lives.

In step five of creating your Personal Change Blueprint, I am asking you to do just that. First, go back and review your outcome, repeat it to yourself a few times and then ask yourself what kind of *sounds* are associated with the accomplishment of your outcome? If you are stuck on this one, I will give you some hints.

An associated sound could be the voice in your head, your internal dialog. It could be comments from other people, or it could be the absence of a particular sound. These sounds can be literal or figurative, and perhaps because you have accomplished this outcome, you hear angels singing or a sigh of relief. Those are both perfectly good answers.

Step Six – Feelings Associated with the Accomplishment of this Outcome

In step six, you will connect with the emotional and physical feelings you notice because you have accomplished your outcome. When you look back at the answers you filled out in your Personal Change Blueprint, and if you are like most of us, you will notice that many of your answers describe feelings.

Not to worry. You do not have to transfer those details to this step on feelings. Just add the new ones. If you feel free, describe what you feel free to do. If you feel happy, describe what you are happy about. If your body feels better because you manifest better health, describe how good it feels and what a relief it is to be free from the old discomfort. This creates much better imagery than saying your feet are not on fire anymore.

Step Seven – What Having this Accomplishment Does for You

Your Personal Change Blueprint is coming along nicely by the time you reach step seven. Before you answer step seven, I ask you to review all the information you have added to your Personal Change Blueprint so far.

You may think of new ideas to add here and there. After you have reviewed your blueprint in its entirety, I want you to sit back and look at the big picture. Look at what you are creating. Look at the magnificence of this change and the ripple effect that comes with it. Now ask yourself what having this accomplishment does for you.

If you were building a new home and designing every square inch of it just the way you wanted, what would having a new home built to your specifications do for you? Why is this creation important? What is the big deal about *this* accomplishment? Take the time to reflect on the value gained by accomplishing the outcome based on this specific subject as you practice your self-hypnosis. This is important.

Step Eight – Influences on the Key Areas of Life

At first glance, it may seem like you have already answered the questions here in step eight. As you work your way through each step and allow yourself to mentally and emotionally experience the perspective of already having what you want, your creativity and imagination will start to flourish. You will notice that more and more details come to you with each step, and it is perfectly fine to go back and add more information to any step you want.

I think of this last step as the domino effect. After all, you get to look at how many things will improve because you are manifesting this one change in your life. And it is an all-positive change.

Step eight allows you to tie up any loose ends by identifying and describing the positive influences you will notice because you have created this change in your life. Here you will be prompted to think about the positive influence on your relationships with family, friends, coworkers, strangers, and so on. You will reflect on the positive influences you will notice regarding your career and finances. When you think of the changes in your health, you will see better emotional, physical, psychological, and intellectual health in many cases. Describe those in detail.

Perhaps the most significant positive influence will be on your self-esteem. How can you feel anything but proud of yourself for accomplishing this outcome and realizing that you now have the key to upgrade any part of your life you want?

And finally, if you have a spiritual practice, you may see a positive influence on the rituals and routines related to your spiritual practice that you enjoy. If you do not have a spiritual practice, no worries, just leave this part blank.

When designing your Personal Change Blueprint, take as little or as much time as you want to answer the questions. In my opinion, this part is more important than practicing self-hypnosis. I recommend taking an hour or so to create your Personal Change Blueprint in one sitting. Then come back to it after a few hours or a day later and review your answers. Feel free to add more detail. There is no hurry to any of this and if filling out one question every day or so works best for you, then do that.

Because you have accomplished your outcome, notice the positive influences in the following areas of your life.

Relationships

- Think about the changes you have made and what kind of positive influence you notice in all your relationships. This includes interactions with friends, family, coworkers, neighbors, and/or strangers.

Career/Finances

- Because of the changes you have made, what kind of positive influence do you notice regarding your career and/or finances? If you are a student, replace career with studies/education. You may notice direct and indirect changes because of having accomplished your outcome.

Health

- This includes physical, mental, and emotional health. Accomplishing personal change almost always improves our health in one or more areas of our life.

Self-Esteem

- Think about how you see yourself in the new light of having accomplished your outcome. How can you describe the positive influence this accomplishment has made on your self-image?

Spirituality

- If you have a spiritual practice, you may notice an "ease" in how you interact with your belief system because of the changes you've made. You may notice a greater sense of freedom and comfort when considering your spiritual practice.

SECTION FOUR

Make It Yours

Chapter Eight

A Template and Some Examples

I will keep these examples simple and have included a Personal Change Blueprint template for you to use. After you have settled on a topic for your self-hypnosis, go through these steps one at a time. Let your imagination step in and show you how amazing your life can be. Your answers will be different than the ones in the examples, and they should be.

The following examples will help you get an idea of how to answer each of the questions in your Personal Change Blueprint. Keep in mind that if you are doing a Personal Change Blueprint for yourself on any of the following topics, your answers will be different, and they should be. Make your blueprint very specific to you and your life experiences.

Your Personal Change Blueprint

© 2022 Intuitive Life Coach and Debbie Taylor

By completing the *eight-step Personal Change Blueprint*, you are choreographing the concepts and words that will be used during your hypnosis or self-hypnosis session so that you achieve maximum benefit. The information you write down on your Personal Change Blueprint will be the words you say back to yourself while you are practicing self-hypnosis. These are your *suggestions*. It is vitally important that you use language that creates the imagery of what you do want.

Step One – Your payoffs and your *now* statement. *These are the words you will say back to yourself while practicing self-hypnosis.*

_____
_____
_____
_____
_____
_____
_____
_____
_____

Step Two – Crafting your desired outcome for exactly what you want. Keep it simple and stated in the positive. This is the focus of your hypnosis session. The information you write down on the remaining steps will be written from the perspective that you have accomplished this outcome. *These are the words you will say back to yourself while practicing self-hypnosis.*

_____
_____
_____
_____
_____
_____
_____
_____

Step Three – Evidence and proof. Ask yourself the following: Because I have accomplished my outcome, what changes do I notice? What *evidence* proves to me that I have made this change? What is different in my daily life? *These are the words you will say back to yourself while practicing self-hypnosis.*

_____
_____
_____
_____
_____
_____
_____

Page 2 – Your Personal Change Blueprint
© 2022 Intuitive Life Coach and Debbie Taylor

Step Four – Imagery: What images come to mind when you think of all the changes in your life because you have accomplished your outcome? *These are the words you will say back to yourself while practicing self-hypnosis.*

_____
_____
_____
_____
_____
_____
_____

Step Five – Sounds: What sounds are associated with having accomplished your outcome? Remember, these can be the voice in your head, comments from others, or the absence of a sound. *These are the words you will say back to yourself while practicing self-hypnosis.*

_____
_____
_____
_____
_____
_____
_____

Step Six – Feelings: What feeling, physical and/or emotional, do you have because you have accomplished your outcome? *These are the words you will say back to yourself while practicing self-hypnosis.*

_____
_____
_____
_____
_____
_____
_____

Step Seven – Summarize all the changes in your life. Because you have accomplished your outcome, ask yourself: What does having achieved this desired outcome do for me? *These are the words you will say back to yourself while practicing self-hypnosis.*

_____
_____
_____
_____
_____
_____
_____
_____
_____
_____

Step Eight – Positive Influences: Because you have accomplished your outcome, you notice positive influences in the following areas. It's okay to write down suggestions you have already written in previous steps.

- Relationships

- Career/Finances

- Health

- Self-esteem

- Spirituality

© 2022 Intuitive Life Coach and Debbie Taylor
Intuitive Life Coach LLC
Portland, Oregon
intuitivelifecoachpublishing.com

Download your free PDF here

The following examples are intended to help you fill out your Personal Change Blueprint by showing possible answers for a variety of topics. You will notice several "re-frame" examples where the original answer was not worded in a way that the imagery created accurately reflects the desired outcome. The reframe examples show you a better way to craft your Personal Change Blueprint by keeping your words and imagery positive.

Example 1 – Self-Hypnosis for Procrastination

Setup – Betty procrastinates all the time, and it has been bothering her for a while now. She always tells herself that she will do better the next day, but she never does. She is not lazy but keeps putting things off and sometimes never does them at all; silly things, like not doing the dishes on time, not keeping her dirty clothes picked up, or even just taking a dirty dish to the sink when she is done with it. This makes her feel bad about herself, and her kids are starting to do the same thing. She has a class she needs to be studying for, and putting it off is stressing her out big time. She cannot seem to make herself get off the couch and get things done. She says, "I need help!"

The following are Betty's answers to the Personal Change Blueprint.

Step One – Your Payoffs and Your *Now* Statement

- *Procrastinating has given me extra time to do things I've enjoyed, like sleeping in a little later, watching more TV, and spending a lot of time on Facebook. It has helped me avoid doing things that are difficult.*
- *It's kept me from taking the risk of failing at things. I appreciate all these benefits, these payoffs; however, I am ready to give up all these payoffs because ...*
- *NOW I am ready to check things off my list. I really do want to accomplish the things I've been putting off. I know that facing my responsibilities like an adult will free up plenty of time for watching TV, and I really don't need or want to waste my life on Facebook anymore. I appreciate all the perceived payoffs for procrastination, but I'm ready to give them up for a life that I feel good about, a life where I take care of business and act like an adult. I'm sick of feeling crappy about myself all the time.*

Step Two – Identifying the Desired Outcome that Explains Exactly What You Want

- *I find it easy to keep up on my to-do list every day and attend to things as soon as I notice or think of them.*

The answer to step two is the focus of this self-hypnosis session.

The answers to all the remaining questions in your Personal Change Blueprint represent the details and results of having accomplished this outcome. Answer the remaining questions as if you had accomplished your outcome on a permanent basis 100% of the time.

Step Three – Your Evidence Because You Have Accomplished this Outcome

- *I set aside 30 min/day to look at Facebook, and I stick to it.*
- *When I change my clothes, I either hang them back up or put them in the dirty clothes hamper.*
- *The dishes get done as soon as I'm done eating. The sink is rinsed out, and the table is wiped off after every meal.*
- *I have time to read while I soak in the tub at the end of the day.*

Step Four – Imagery Associated with the Accomplishment of this Outcome

- *I see myself going over my task list for the day every morning as I enjoy that first cup of coffee.*
- *My floor is clean, and I see the carpet because all the dirty clothes are in the hamper.*
- *My kitchen is clean, and the dishwasher is full of dishes.*
- *I see my kids putting their dirty dishes in the dishwasher after every meal.*
- *I see myself signing up to take classes and doing things I want to do.*

Step Five – Sounds Associated with the Accomplishment of this Outcome

- *I hear the dishwasher running at night right after dinner has been cleaned up.*
- *I hear my favorite music on in the background while I'm attending to daily tasks as they come up.*
- *The voice in my head is kind, and I'm praising myself for taking care of tasks on the spot.*
- *My partner is thanking me for keeping my dirty clothes picked up.*

Step Six – Feelings Associated with the Accomplishment of this Outcome

- *It feels good to have my house picked up on a regular basis.*
- *I'm comfortable knowing that if someone drops by unannounced, my house is presentable.*
- *I love the feeling of waking up to a clean kitchen and a dishwasher full of clean dishes every morning.*
- *I look forward to looking at my daily to-do list because checking things off that list every day feels really good and actually leaves me with more time for TV, guilt-free TV time!*
- *I feel like an adult in charge of my environment, and it feels good knowing that I'm doing a great job.*

Step Seven – What Does Having this Accomplishment Do for You?

- *This change allows me to move beyond the daily routine that became a habit when I was in college and living alone for the first time.*
- *Now I can go to that next step. Having my physical environment cleaned up, I have the mental and emotional freedom to do what's next in my life.*

Step Eight – Positive Influences on Key Areas of Life

Relationships

- *I feel more inclined to invite people over to my house.*
- *The relationship I have with myself feels more grown-up.*
- *Because I feel better about myself, I feel more confident when interacting with other people.*
- *My partner sees me and treats me like an equal rather than an unruly child.*

Career/Finances

- *Part of my daily tasks is keeping up with my budget.*
- *I feel more relaxed about my bank balance.*
- *When I go to the store now, I am free from any worry that I am spending too much because I take the time to check my balance before leaving the house. My head is out of the sand!*

> **Reframe** *so that the imagery created accurately reflects what is wanted.*
>
> *Reframe* **"free from any worry that I am spending too much"** *to something like* **"am confident in my spending."**
>
> *Therefore, the entire reframed sentence would be:*
>
> **When I go to the store now, I am confident in my spending because I take the time to check my balance before leaving the house. My head is out of the sand!**

- *My new habit of taking care of daily tasks around the house is taking hold at work too. I am staying on task consistently and attending to my responsibilities as they come up. At the end of my workday, I can leave work at work.*

Health

- *I feel so much better about myself. This makes it easy to eat right and get outside for more physical activity. And I have the time to do it too!*
- *I am sleeping better just knowing that I will wake up in the morning to a clean house, a dishwasher full of clean dishes, and best of all, I wake up every morning free from dread.*

Self-Esteem

- *My self-esteem has improved a great deal. I like this version of me, and I plan to keep things going like this.*
- *I feel more grown-up, more authentic. I am a responsible adult, and this is real. It is who I am now. Finally!*

Spirituality

- *Now when I meditate, it is from an authentic desire to do so. I used to use it as an escape. There is nothing to escape from now. The connection I feel to my higher self is a beautiful thing. I am grateful to myself for making this change.*

> **Reframe** *so the imagery created accurately reflects what is wanted.*
>
> *Reframe* **"I used to use it as an escape. There is nothing to escape from now."** *It can be omitted.*
>
> *Therefore, the entire reframed sentence would be:*
>
> **Now when I meditate, it is from an authentic desire to do so. The connection I feel to my higher self is a beautiful thing. I am grateful to myself for making this change.**

Example 2 – Self-Hypnosis for Sleep

Setup – Roger has not had a full night's sleep for so long it feels like it has been forever. He guesses it all started when his marriage fell apart. He hated going to bed because he would just lay there and toss and turn and worry. Then once he did fall asleep, he would wake up in a panic every couple of hours. Roger tried drinking wine right before bed, which sometimes helped, but then he would have headaches and start gaining weight. He does not want to take prescription medication, but he *has* to do something. Roger needs to get some sleep. This is affecting every part of his life, and not in a good way.

The following are Roger's answers to the Personal Change Blueprint.

Step One – Your Payoffs and Your *Now* Statement

- *The sleeping habit I am saying goodbye to is one that started years ago when my spouse asked for a divorce. I would stay up all night crying and worrying about my future. I understand now that my subconscious mind was keeping me up at all hours of the night to give me a chance to process this turn of events and to problem-solve. I want to thank my subconscious mind for this opportunity, but the divorce happened years ago, and I no longer need help trying to figure this out. This situation is over, and it is not relevant to my life right now. So, I am saying thanks, but I do not need this anymore because . . .*

- *NOW, all those questions I had at that time have been answered. All the problems going on back then have been solved. It is not happening anymore. Now my life is in a good place, and if I ever need time to figure stuff out, I do it best during the daylight hours, after I have had a full night's sleep.*

Step Two – Identifying the Desired Outcome that Explains Exactly What You Want

- *I find it easy to drift off into a deep sleep within minutes of closing my eyes to enjoy a full night of unbroken sleep every single night!*

The answer to step two is the focus of this self-hypnosis session.

The answers to all the remaining questions in your blueprint represent the details, the results of having accomplished this outcome. Answer the remaining questions in your Personal Change Blueprint as if you had accomplished your outcome on a permanent basis 100% of the time.

Step Three – Your Evidence Because You Have Accomplished this Outcome

- *I wake up every morning feeling refreshed, satisfied, and eager for the day.*
- *I like waking up early enough each morning to do a thirty-minute workout.*

- *It is easy for me to stay on task at work. My mind is clear, focused, and alert all day.*
- *I have energy for my family when I get home each day.*
- *It is easy to eat right.*
- *I am in a better mood and more fun to be around.*

> **Reframe** *so that the imagery created accurately reflects what is wanted.*
>
> *Reframe* **"I am in a better mood"** *to* **"I am in a great mood."**
>
> *Therefore, the entire reframed sentence would be:*
>
> **"I am in a great mood and more fun to be around."**

Step Four – Imagery Associated with the Accomplishment of this Outcome

- *I can see myself bounding out of bed in the morning, fully awake and ready for the day.*
- *I am losing weight because I have time and energy to work out every day now.*
- *I see myself driving to work with a look of contentment on my face, looking forward to the day's activities.*
- *I see myself socializing more. I am having fun out with my friends.*

- *I see myself accepting invitations to go out and do things with my friends on a regular basis.*

Step Five – Sounds Associated with the Accomplishment of this Outcome

- *My kids tell me it is nice to have me in a good mood in the mornings.*
- *The voice in my head is rattling off all the fun things I can do next: taking classes, calling friends, decorating my home.*
- *I am singing along to the music in my car on the way to work every day.*
- *My partner is talking to me and telling me it is nice to see me happy for once.*

Step Six – Feelings Associated with the Accomplishment of this Outcome

- *I feel alive again.*
- *I feel very happy about my life; everything is going so well.*
- *I feel bouncy, silly, almost giddy with joyfulness, for no reason at all.*
- *I find it easy to eat right and exercise, and I am relieved to be taking care of my health again.*

Step Seven – What Does Having this Accomplishment Do for You?

- *This gives my life back to me and me back to my family.*

- *This sets the stage for me to enjoy life and make plans about what I can do next.*
- *Being in survival is a thing of the past. I am in creative mode now!*
- *I look forward to the future. It feels bright, joyful, and beautiful.*

Step Eight – Positive Influences on Key Areas of Life

Relationships

- *People at work and home can be around me with ease.*
- *I enjoy spending time with people.*
- *I am very patient when listening to my kids.*
- *I am more helpful to my kids and people at work.*
- *My interactions and connections with people are more authentic.*

> ***Reframe*** *so that the imagery created accurately reflects what is wanted.*
>
> *Reframe* **"with people are more authentic"** *to* **"with people are authentic,"** *removing the word more.*
>
> *Therefore, the entire reframed sentence would be:*
>
> **"My interactions and connections with people are authentic."**

Career/Finances

- *I am using my time at work very efficiently now. I am approachable, available, and sincerely enjoy helping my team.*
- *I initiate team gatherings and enjoy being part of the organization I work for.*
- *My managers see me in a new light. I would not be surprised to find out that I am being considered for promotion because I offer so much value at work. This translates into more money and a promotion.*

Health

- *Because I am sleeping well every night, my body can take advantage of my healthy eating habits and my daily workouts. I am losing weight.*
- *My immune system is no longer compromised from lack of sleep, and it is strong and vibrant, just like me.*

> **Reframe** so that the imagery created accurately reflects what is wanted.
>
> Reframe **"system is no longer compromised from lack of sleep"** by deleting the negative reminder.
>
> Therefore, the entire reframed sentence would be:
>
> **"My immune system is strong and vibrant, just like me."**

- *My emotional health is much better.*

> **Reframe** *so that the imagery created accurately reflects what is wanted.*
>
> *Reframe "**is much better**" by replacing the words "much better" with the desired outcome.*
>
> *Therefore, the entire reframed sentence would be:*
>
> **"My emotional health is good because I keep problems in perspective. I feel good about myself."**

Self-Esteem

- *I like myself again. The internal dialog I have about myself is all positive.*

> **Reframe** *so that the imagery created accurately reflects what is wanted.*
>
> *Reframe "**I like myself again**" by removing the word "again."*
>
> *Therefore, the entire reframed sentence would be:*
>
> **"I like myself. The internal dialog I have about myself is all positive."**

- *I am proud of the changes I have made in my life, I love my life, and I have myself to thank for all of this.*
- *I AM a good person. I trust my decisions; I know what I am doing. I am free from any sense of being less-than.*

Spirituality

- *I can stay awake while meditating now.*
- *I am back in touch with the feeling of gratitude which is a very spiritual thing for me.*
- *I know that if I attend the spiritual retreat I am interested in, I will get a lot from it because I will be alert and awake and present for all of it.*

Example 3 – Self-Hypnosis for Test Anxiety

Setup – Jane has always been a good student. She gets good grades on all her assignments, and her homework is always turned in on time. She easily passes any quiz she takes, and her teachers have nothing but positive feedback about her progress. However, every time she has a major test to take, she caves in. She does not know what happens. Jane's mind goes blank, and her heart starts racing; she is sweaty and nauseous and cannot finish the test in time. She is so frustrated! Jane needs to pass this next test so she can advance to the next level in her program. The more she thinks about it, the worse it gets. She asks, "What is going on?"

The following are Jane's answers to the Personal Change Blueprint.

Step One – Your Payoffs and Your *Now* Statement

- *I have come to understand that having anxiety about taking a test is my subconscious mind's way of keeping me from taking a test so that I can avoid the risk of failure, and for some reason, it thinks it is helping me. Wow! It is not helping at all. I am always well prepared for any test I take. Subconscious mind, I am ready to take the risk of failure and give up this test anxiety because . . .*
- *NOW I know I will pass the exam I have been studying for. I am beyond prepared for this. I understand all the material. I study all the time. No one is better prepared than I am. I have done well with all the homework and quizzes. I have important things to do in my life, and keeping me safe from some imagined failure is a joke.*

Step Two – Identifying the Desired Outcome that Explains Exactly What You Want

- *I find it easy to remain calm and focused while taking this or any exam. I feel 100% confident in my ability to pass with a high score. I am relaxed, at ease, and focused before, during, and after the exam.*

The answer to step two is the focus of this self-hypnosis session.

The answers to all the remaining questions in your blueprint represent the details, the results of having accomplished this outcome. Answer the remaining questions in your Personal Change Blueprint as if you had accomplished your outcome on a permanent basis 100% of the time.

Step Three – Your Evidence Because You Have Accomplished this Outcome

- *I remain calm even when anticipating going to the exam room.*
- *While taking the test, my heart rate is so normal I do not even notice it.*
- *When I read each question, it is easy to know exactly what they are asking for.*
- *It is easy to stay focused on what I am doing during the exam.*
- *I am free from distraction and completely present.*

> ***Reframe*** *so that the imagery created accurately reflects what is wanted.*
>
> *Reframe* **"I am free from distraction"** *by removing the negative phrase.*
>
> *Therefore, the entire reframed sentence would be:*
>
> **"I am focused and completely present."**

Step Four – Imagery Associated with the Accomplishment of this Outcome

- *I see myself entering the testing room with absolute calmness.*
- *I see myself finishing the exam a little early.*
- *I see myself checking over the answers and feeling really good about all of them.*
- *When I look at the multiple-choice answers to choose from, it is like the right answer is blinking at me; it is so obvious.*
- *I see myself opening the email with my test scores and seeing a really good score.*
- *There is an ease to my demeanor before, during, and after I take the test.*

Step Five – Sounds Associated with the Accomplishment of this Outcome

- *The voice in my head is calm and reassuring.*
- *I am reading the questions to myself, and I know the answer before I even look at the choices.*
- *It is quiet. I am oblivious to any other sounds in the room.*
- *The sound of my breathing is normal, so normal I do not even think about what it sounds like.*
- *I hear myself silently squealing with delight when I finish, and I am turning in my test a few minutes early.*
- *Once I get back in my car where no one can hear me, I am cheering out loud!*

- *I hear myself telling my parents and friends how well I did and that I am proud of myself and excited for the next step in my studies.*

Step Six – Feelings Associated with the Accomplishment of this Outcome

- *I feel very proud of myself.*
- *I am excited about my future, and now I can move forward with the next step in this process.*
- *I feel like celebrating another success in my life.*
- *I feel very confident about passing this exam, and the next, and the next.*

Step Seven – What Does Having this Accomplishment Do for You?

- *The skill of remaining calm, focused, and confident under pressure is one that will follow me into many other areas of life, especially grad school and then my career.*
- *This is going to set me up for success when it is time to interview for jobs.*

> ***Reframe*** *so that the imagery created accurately reflects what is wanted.*
>
> *Reframe* **"This is going to"** *by changing the words* **"going to"** *to* **"I am set up."**
>
> *Therefore, the entire reframed sentence would be:*

> *"I am set up for success when it is time to interview for jobs."*

- *I am really good at my work because I can think clearly and solve problems very efficiently.*

Step Eight – Positive Influences on Key Areas of Life

Relationships

- *My friends are proud of me and are comfortable bringing up the subject of my test score because I have done so well.*
- *I am free from that black cloud of doubt and confusion that used to follow me around. This makes me more fun to be around!*

> **Reframe** *so that the imagery created accurately reflects what is wanted.*
>
> *Reframe* **"I am free from that black cloud of doubt and confusion that used to follow me around"** *by omitting the negative reference and replacing it with the desired outcome. For example:* **"I am enjoying the blue skies of confidence and clarity."**
>
> *Therefore, the entire reframed sentence would be:*

> *"I am enjoying the blue skies of confidence and clarity. This makes me fun to be around!"*

- *My confidence makes me more attractive and approachable.*

> ***Reframe*** *so that the imagery created accurately reflects what is wanted.*
>
> *Reframe* **"makes me more attractive"** *by omitting the word "more."*
>
> *Therefore, the entire reframed sentence would be:*
>
> ***"My confidence makes me attractive and approachable."***

Career/Finances

- *My confidence shines through in a job interview, and the people I work with at school see me as a very capable, confident person.*
- *My managers see that I am smart, confident, and very good at what I do.*
- *I climb the ladder of success, making more money every step of the way.*

Health

- *I am so happy and relieved about my ability to stay calm whenever I take a test that it is easy to sleep well every night.*
- *Getting adequate sleep makes it easier to eat right and exercise every day.*
- *I feel more in control of my life and notice a huge decrease in my stress levels.*

Self-Esteem

- *I am very happy to be demonstrating to the world what I have always believed to be true about myself, that I am smart, capable, and able to score high on any exam I take.*
- *I am proud of myself and feel great confidence in my ability to enter into a challenging work field.*
- *I have great faith in my ability to do whatever I choose. Not only have I learned to remain calm and focused while taking a test, but I also passed the test with a very good score. This is a double win, and I feel really, really good about myself. I am all that!*

Spirituality

- *I do not really have a spiritual practice, but if I did, I would be happy thinking that I am living up to my God-given potential.*

Example 4 – Self-Hypnosis for Public Speaking Anxiety

Setup – Danny goes into an absolute panic with the mere thought of having to participate in meetings at work. It is not just standing on a stage in front of an audience that gets to him, although that completely freaks him out. It is the idea of being called on, out of the blue, put on the spot. Danny's mind goes blank, and he feels numb and tingly. He cannot think straight, and his face feels like it is on fire. Danny cannot even think about this now without having a panic attack. It honestly makes him sick to his stomach. He has to get over this. He is really good at what he does at work, he is smart, and he has a lot to contribute, but for some reason, it scares Danny to death when he thinks of having to speak up at meetings. He asks, "How do people do it?"

The following are Danny's answers to the Personal Change Blueprint.

Step One – Your Payoffs and Your *Now* Statement

- *I have come to understand that having anxiety attacks around the idea of public speaking is just my subconscious mind's way of keeping me from doing something that could be embarrassing, something I could fail at, something that scares me, and it keeps me safe from being judged from others. I get it, and I appreciate all this supposed benefit of public speaking anxiety, but I do not want it anymore. It is not helping. I am ready to thank it, bless it, and send it on its way because . . .*

- *NOW I want to speak in front of groups! I have so much to offer and teach. I want to look forward to sharing my expertise with others. I am confident about what I have to say, and I know my input will be well received. Subconscious mind, I am ready to take the risk of putting myself out there by speaking in public. The time has come.*

Step Two – Identifying the Desired Outcome that Explains Exactly What You Want

- *I find it easy to remain calm, focused, and clear-headed anytime I have the chance to speak in public, whether in front of a small group or a large audience.*

The answer to step two is the focus of this self-hypnosis session.

The answers to all the remaining questions in your blueprint represent the details, the results of having accomplished this outcome. Answer the remaining questions in your Personal Change Blueprint as if you had accomplished your outcome on a permanent basis 100% of the time.

Step Three – Your Evidence Because You Have Accomplished this Outcome

- *I look forward to speaking engagements.*
- *I willingly accept offers to present in small and/or large groups.*

- *I am always prepared to share my knowledge.*
- *My presentations are well received, and I get very positive feedback from others.*
- *If I am put on the spot in a meeting, I remain calm and focused as I respond with confidence and clarity.*

Step Four – Imagery Associated with the Accomplishment of this Outcome

- *I see myself on stage so wrapped up in what I am talking about that I forget I was ever nervous about speaking in public.*

> **Reframe** *so that the imagery created accurately reflects what is wanted.*
>
> *Reframe* **"that I forget I was ever nervous about speaking in public,"** *therefore not focusing on the negative and instead focusing on the positive. For example,* **"I see myself on stage wrapped up in what I am talking about and confident about speaking in public."**
>
> *Therefore, the entire reframed sentence would be:*
>
> **"I see myself on stage wrapped up in what I am talking about and confident about speaking in public."**

- *I am making eye contact with my audience, and I have them in the palm of my hand.*
- *I have the look of a very seasoned and confident speaker.*
- *I have good posture, perfect mannerisms, the right pace, and everything looks so natural.*
- *I am physically relaxed and present.*

Step Five – Sounds Associated with the Accomplishment of this Outcome

- *As I am waiting to go on stage, I can hear the sound of my introduction as I tune into how calm I feel.*
- *I hear applause as I go onto the stage and give a wave of hello to my audience.*
- *Whether I am on a stage or sitting around a conference table at work, when I speak, my voice sounds strong, calm, confident, and clear.*
- *The pace and volume of my voice are very professional.*
- *My confidence puts my audience at ease.*
- *The voice in my head is very happy and full of positive comments.*
- *I hear excellent feedback about my contribution or presentation.*
- *I am invited to speak at upcoming events, and I hear myself eagerly accepting those invitations.*

Step Six – Feelings Associated with the Accomplishment of this Outcome

- *I feel so proud of myself for being able to do this.*
- *I feel so relieved as I listen to the strength of my voice.*

- *I am excited to be sharing my expertise in a way that adds value to the lives of others.*
- *I feel more professional, more elevated as a mover and shaker in the community.*

> **Reframe** so that the imagery created accurately reflects what is wanted.
>
> Reframe *"***I feel more professional, more elevated,***" removing the word "more." For example, "****I feel professional and elevated.****"*
>
> *Therefore, the entire reframed sentence would be:*
>
> **"I feel professional and elevated as a mover and shaker in the community."**

Step Seven – What Does Having this Accomplishment Do for You?

- *This elevates my status in the organization I work for, which is huge.*
- *I am setting myself up for promotions. People are noticing me as someone who stands out in a good way.*
- *People come to me for advice, and they value my contribution.*

Step Eight – Positive Influences on Key Areas of Life

Relationships

- *My work relationships are more professional. People see me as an expert and seek my input on important issues.*

> **Reframe** *so that the imagery created accurately reflects what is wanted.*
>
> *Reframe* **"are more professional,"** *removing the word "more." For example,* **"My work relationships are professional."**
>
> *Therefore, the entire reframed sentence would be:*
>
> **"My work relationships are professional. People see me as an expert and seek my input on important issues."**

- *My increased confidence makes me more approachable. People like to be around me and hear what I have to say.*
- *I feel like I am being taken seriously now.*
- *I feel confident about providing for my family.*

Career/Finances

- *I have opportunities to travel for work. I like to travel, and now it is paid for.*
- *I stand out among my coworkers as someone who can elevate the mission of the entire organization.*
- *I earn more money because my skill level has increased.*

> **Reframe** *so that the imagery created accurately reflects what is wanted.*
>
> *Reframe* **"I earn more money,"** *replacing the word "more." For example,* **"I earn lots of money."**
>
> *Reframe* **"has increased,"** *replacing from past to present.*
>
> *Therefore, the entire reframed sentence would be:*
>
> **"I earn lots of money because my skill level is increasing."**

- *I have more options if I choose to interview for different positions within or outside my current organization.*

> **Reframe** *so that the imagery created accurately reflects what is wanted.*
>
> *Reframe* **"I have more options if I choose,"** *replacing the word "more." For example,* **"I have lots of options."**
>
> *Therefore, the entire reframed sentence would be:*
>
> **"I have lots of options to interview for different positions within or outside my current organization."**

Health

- *I sleep well at night, knowing that as I anticipate speaking in any situation, I do so with absolute calmness and am able to remain clear-headed and very focused.*
- *Because I feel better about myself, I am finding it easy to eat right and be more physically active.*
- *I am losing weight and enjoy fitting into nice work clothes.*

Self-Esteem

- *I am free from the black cloud of doubt and frustration.*

> **Reframe** *so that the imagery created accurately reflects what is wanted.*
>
> *Reframe* **"I am free from the black cloud of doubt and frustration,"** *replacing the negative phrase with the desired outcome. For example,* **"I enjoy the clear blue skies of confidence and delight/ pleasure/ joy."**
>
> *Therefore, the entire reframed sentence would be:*
>
> **"I enjoy the clear blue skies of confidence and joy."**

- *The positive feedback I get from my speaking engagements seems to trigger ideas and ways to add value.*
- *My confidence has gone through the roof!*
- *I am proud of my accomplishments and feel like the sky is the limit.*

Spirituality

- *I enjoy participating in study groups related to spirituality, and I feel calm and relaxed when I have something to add to the conversation.*
- *I feel confident when I think about putting on a workshop or running a course related to my spiritual beliefs.*

Example 5 – Self-Hypnosis for Weight Loss

Setup – Elizabeth is so sick and tired of thinking about food all the time. It seems like all she does is think about what to eat next or how much she hates herself for what she just ate. She sees herself as fat and lazy, and she does not get it. Elizabeth has tried everything under the sun to lose weight. She can lose it; she just cannot keep it off. It is like some invisible force takes over Elizabeth's brain, and she cannot stay away from fast food joints, sweets, or chips. Elizabeth feels out of control! She feels like the only person in the world who cannot lose weight. Elizabeth hates looking in the mirror. She does not know how her husband can stand looking at her. Elizabeth wants to be a normal-sized person, but she does not know what to do.

The following are Elizabeth's answers to the Personal Change Blueprint.

Step One – Your Payoffs and Your *Now* Statement

- *My current eating habits have given me the freedom to eat what I want, when I want, where I want, as much as I want, if I want. I enjoy freedom, but the weight gain has made me a prisoner of my own life. I am willing to relinquish this freedom in exchange for a set of personal boundaries in regard to my eating habits because . . .*
- *. . . NOW I want to have the freedom to wear cute clothes. I want the freedom of feeling comfortable out in public. I want to focus on something other than the next thing I am going to eat. I want to be naturally healthy and fit.*

Step Two – Identifying the Desired Outcome that Explains Exactly What You Want

- *I enjoy having an adult relationship with food and eating healthy, nutritious foods in just the right amounts at just the right times, every single day, no matter where I am or who else is around.*

The answer to step two is the focus of this self-hypnosis session.

The answers to all the remaining questions in your blueprint represent the details, the results of having accomplished this outcome. Answer the remaining questions in your Personal Change Blueprint as if you had accomplished your outcome on a permanent basis 100% of the time.

Step Three – Your Evidence Because You Have Accomplished this Outcome

- *I spend three minutes each week planning the meals and snacks I will have for that week.*
- *I make a grocery list based on the list of meals and snacks I have decided on, and I stick to it.*
- *When I get home from grocery shopping, I do some batch cooking and food prep, and I am ready for the week.*
- *My body is changing shape, and my clothes are getting baggy on me.*
- *I enjoy being free from the constant obsession with what I am going to eat next.*

> **Reframe** *so that the imagery created accurately reflects what is wanted.*
>
> *Reframe* **"free from,"** *replacing the negative phrase with the desired outcome. For example,* **"I enjoy knowing when my next meal will be."**
>
> *Therefore, the entire reframed sentence would be:*
>
> **"I enjoy knowing when my next meal will be and following through on waiting for it."**

- *I am free from regret when it comes to my eating habits.*

> *Reframe so that the imagery created accurately reflects what is wanted.*
>
> *Reframe* **"free from,"** *replacing the negative phrase with the desired outcome. For example,* **"I enjoy contentment."**
>
> *Therefore, the entire reframed sentence would be:*
>
> **"I am content and pleased and proud of myself when it comes to my healthy eating habits."**

- *I am eating single-size portions, and they are more than enough to satisfy me.*

Step Four – Imagery Associated with the Accomplishment of this Outcome

- *My grocery cart is full of fruits and vegetables and healthy lean meats.*
- *I am only buying the things on the grocery list I made when I was planning my meals and snacks for the week.*
- *I see myself completely ignoring the drive-up windows I used to go to.*
- *When I look in the mirror, I see my face looking different, slimmer.*

- *When I see my reflection in the glass doors at the store, I look like a normal person.*
- *I see myself walking a little faster, and I have more bounce to my step.*
- *It is easier to pick things up off the floor.*
- *I can see muscle definition in my arms and legs, and my stomach is shrinking!*

Step Five – Sounds Associated with the Accomplishment of this Outcome

- *I hear compliments from other people about my weight loss.*
- *I hear my partner telling me he's proud of me.*
- *I hear the voice in my head saying delete every time I even think about going back to my old way of eating.*
- *I hear that little voice in my head squealing with delight as I am shopping for new clothes and looking for things that fit me on the normal size racks.*
- *I hear the sound of my breath, very strong and healthy, as I am working out or riding my bike.*
- *My mind is quiet. There is a clear absence of regret when I get in the car to go home after I have attended an event where there was a lot of food available.*
- *I hear the sound of relief when I step on the scales.*
- *I hear my doctor expressing her approval and happiness for my progress.*

Step Six – Feelings Associated with the Accomplishment of this Outcome

- *I am over the moon with happiness and pride!*
- *I am so relieved that I have finally found the answer to my weight loss problems.*
- *I am 100% confident in my ability to maintain my progress. This is permanent weight loss.*
- *I feel grateful knowing that I am going to live a long and healthy life free from any weight-related health concerns.*
- *I feel sexy! Attractive! Frisky!*

Step Seven – What Does Having this Accomplishment Do for You?

- *This is a huge game-changer for me. Losing this weight proves to me that I can do anything and everything I set my mind to.*
- *It proves to me that I can have the kind of life I envision for myself.*
- *Now I know I am going to live a long and healthy life.*
- *I am free from worrying about becoming a diabetic.*

> **Reframe** *so that the imagery created accurately reflects what is wanted.*
>
> *Reframe "**free from,**" replacing the negative phrase with the desired outcome. For example, "**I enjoy contentment.**"*

> *Therefore, the entire reframed sentence would be:*
>
> ***"I am content and pleased and proud of myself when it comes to my healthy eating habits."***

Step Eight – Positive Influences on Key Areas of Life

Relationships

- *I feel like a better partner and a better parent to my kids because I am modeling the behavior of someone that had a serious weight problem and took control of it.*
- *I enjoy intimacy much more, which makes for a closer relationship with my partner.*
- *My relationship with myself is clean and pure. No more beating myself up over my weight.*

> **Reframe** *so that the imagery created accurately reflects what is wanted.*
>
> *Reframe* **"No more beating myself up,"** *replacing the negative phrase with the desired outcome. For example,* **"patting myself on the back."**
>
> *Therefore, the entire reframed sentence would be:*

> *"My relationship with myself is clean and pure, and I am proudly patting myself on the back."*

Career/Finances

- *I think people take me more seriously at work. They are not distracted by my obesity; they actually hear what I have to say.*

> **Reframe** *so that the imagery created accurately reflects what is wanted.*
>
> *Reframe* **"me more seriously,"** *removing "more."*
>
> *Reframe* **"They are not distracted by my obesity; they actually hear what I have to say."**
>
> *Therefore, the entire reframed sentence would be:*
>
> **"People take me seriously at work. They are attracted to what I am saying and hear what I have to say."**

- *I feel and look more professional, and it shows in the way I present myself and my work.*

> **Reframe** *so that the imagery created accurately reflects what is wanted.*

> *Reframe **"more professional,"** removing "more."*
>
> *Therefore, the entire reframed sentence would be:*
>
> ***"I feel and look professional, and it shows in the way I present myself and my work."***

- *My work clothes look very attractive on me.*
- *I have a lot of physical and emotional energy, and it is easy to stay on task. I am an excellent employee and have very high job satisfaction.*
- *I get more done in less time. My managers see that I am a good candidate for promotion.*

Health

- *I am sleeping better. It is just easier to sleep well when I can roll over with ease and wake up feeling good about myself.*
- *Because I am eating better, I am finding it easier to work out regularly.*
- *My stress levels have decreased a great deal, and my doctor will be adjusting the medication I take for high blood pressure and depression.*

> **Reframe** *so that the imagery created accurately reflects what is wanted.*
>
> Reframe *"**stress levels have decreased**" to "**My level of calm has increased.**"*
>
> *Therefore, the entire reframed sentence would be:*
>
> *"**My level of calm has increased a great deal, and my doctor will be adjusting the medication I take for high blood pressure and depression.**"*

Self-Esteem

- *I like the person I see in the mirror now.*
- *My self-esteem and personal confidence have gone through the roof!*
- *Because I exude happiness and confidence, it is easier to be out in public, and I am making new friends.*
- *People see the real me, and it is easy for me to be authentic. I have nothing to hide or feel embarrassed about.*

> **Reframe** *so that the imagery created accurately reflects what is wanted.*

> *Reframe* **"I have nothing to hide or feel embarrassed about,"** *removing the negative. For example,* **"I have everything to SHOW and feel CONFIDENT about."**
>
> *Therefore, the entire reframed sentence would be:*
>
> **"People see the real me, and it is easy for me to be authentic. I have everything to SHOW and feel CONFIDENT about."**

Spirituality

- *I find it easy to sit in meditation for longer periods of time.*
- *I like going to yoga.*
- *I feel a deeper spiritual connection with my higher self because I am honoring and respecting this body I live in.*
- *My gratitude levels are up. The more I express gratitude for my blessings, the more blessings I have to be grateful for!*

Example 6 – Self-Hypnosis for Smoking

Setup – Sean has tried to quit smoking so many times. He has used the gum, the patches, the prescriptions, and cold turkey. Sean has been able to quit for a few weeks here and there, but then he caves in and goes back to it. "It is so frustrating! How do people do it?" he asks. Sean feels he is a strong person but cannot give up "this damn habit." He is embarrassed about being a smoker and hates the idea of people finding out that he smokes. Sean tries to hide it. After he has a cigarette, Sean washes his hands, chews gum, and sprays cologne all over himself. Sean hates going to restaurants with friends and being the only one who has to get up in the middle of a conversation to stand out on the corner in the rain, so he can have a cigarette. Then he goes back to the table where his friends are, and this cloud of stink is following him. The conversation has carried on without him, and he feels like a loser. He hates this! Sean has serious concerns about his health as he enters retirement age. "This has to stop, but how?" Sean asks.

The following are Sean's answers to the Personal Change Blueprint.

Step One – Your Payoffs and Your *Now* Statement

- *When I created the habit of smoking, it was fun. I was young and enjoyed the feeling of being rebellious and doing things I should not have been doing. When I learned to smoke, it was in a very festive party environment with great music, great friends, great beer, cute girls, and a very carefree lifestyle. I am glad I had fun back in the day, but I am here to give up the habit of smoking because . . .*

- *NOW I do not need to smoke to have friends or listen to great music. Smoking is not fun at all anymore. It is expensive, smelly, and disgusting. I am not a kid anymore, and there is absolutely no value in smoking. None whatsoever. I am ready to be free from the smoking habit forever.*

Step Two – Identifying the Desired Outcome that Explains Exactly What You Want

- *I enjoy being a natural non-smoker, free from any thought or desire to smoke cigarettes for the rest of my long and healthy life.*

The answer to step two is the focus of this self-hypnosis session.

The answers to all the remaining questions in your blueprint represent the details, the results of having accomplished this outcome. Answer the remaining questions in your Personal Change Blueprint as if you had accomplished your outcome on a permanent basis 100% of the time.

Step Three – Your Evidence Because You Have Accomplished this Outcome

- *I have $300/month extra in my pocket every single month now, and this is every month for the rest of my life! I can save this money for retirement. I can save it and spoil my grandkids for Christmas every year. I could save it and take a vacation to Hawaii or Mexico. If I want a new car, I can use this money for a car payment. Wow! I have traded in a crappy habit for a free car. That is a great trade!*
- *I feel comfortable out in public now, free from any self-consciousness about smelling like an ashtray if I am standing next to someone in line.*

> **Reframe** *so that the imagery created accurately reflects what is wanted.*
>
> *Reframe* **"free from any self-consciousness about smelling like an ashtray,"** *removing the negative reference. For example,* **"I smell clean and fresh."**
>
> *Therefore, the entire reframed sentence would be:*
>
> **"I feel comfortable out in public now, smelling clean and fresh."**

- *My partner lets me kiss her as much as I want now!*

- *I enjoy being able to sit at a restaurant engrossed in great conversation with my friends or family and being able to stay inside the whole time, where it is warm and dry.*
- *I belong to the group of non-smokers now.*
- *My patio is clean and free from any evidence of a filthy disgusting habit.*
- *My car smells fresh and clean. If someone needs a ride somewhere, I am perfectly comfortable with the idea of offering them a ride.*
- *I have more time to do things I value, like reading, crafts, and spending quality time with my kids and grandkids.*
- *It is easy to work out because I can breathe! I am getting stronger, and I am compelled to eat right and work out regularly.*

Step Four – Imagery Associated with the Accomplishment of this Outcome

- *I see myself telling my doctor I am a non-smoker, and she gives me a big hug.*
- *I see myself living to a ripe old age, free from any worry about tobacco-related health concerns.*

> ***Reframe*** *so that the imagery created accurately reflects what is wanted.*
>
> *Reframe* **"free from any worry,"** *removing the negative reference and replacing it with the desired outcome. For example,* **"as healthy as is possible."**
>
> *Therefore, the entire reframed sentence would be:*

> *"I see myself living to a ripe old age as healthy as is possible."*

- *I see myself traveling with ease. I feel free from concern if my flight is delayed and I have to spend extra time in the boarding area.*
- *I see my partner's face with a big smile. No more concern about me getting cancer from smoking, and no more nagging about the smell!*

> **Reframe** *so that the imagery created accurately reflects what is wanted.*
>
> *Reframe* **"No more concern about me getting cancer from smoking, and no more nagging about the smell!"** *removing the negative reference and replacing it with the desired outcome. For example,* **"as healthy as is possible."**
>
> *Therefore, the entire reframed sentence would be:*
>
> **"I see my partner's face with a big smile. I am proud of healthy activities and how clean and fresh I smell!"**

Step Five – Sounds Associated with the Accomplishment of this Outcome

- *I hear good reports from my doctor and dentist.*
- *I hear the laughter of my kids and grandkids when we are out camping or biking and having fun.*
- *I hear the voice in my head, noticing all the experiences I get to have now because I get to stay put. No more sneaking away.*

> **Reframe** *so that the imagery created accurately reflects what is wanted.*
>
> *Reframe* **"No more sneaking away"** *by removing the negative reference and replacing it with the desired outcome. For example,* **"staying present"** *or deleted completely.*
>
> *Therefore, the entire reframed sentence would be:*
>
> **"I hear the voice in my head, noticing all the experiences I get to have now because I get to stay put."**

- *I hear the sound of a very healthy cardiovascular system when I am lifting weights or running or biking.*

Step Six – Feelings Associated with the Accomplishment of this Outcome

- *I am so proud of myself that I could burst.*
- *I feel a huge sense of relief to know that I will live a long and healthy life free from any tobacco-related health concerns.*
- *I feel smart and free and grown-up.*
- *I am free from feeling like a low life hanging out on the corner in the rain. I am free to stay where it is warm and dry, and I am happy and healthy.*
- *I feel like I am in control of my daily routine now.*
- *I feel bright, shiny, and clean as a whistle from top to bottom. My hair smells good, my breath smells good, my car smells good, my hands smell good, and my clothes smell good. I smell good! And I can smell good things too!*

Step Seven – What Does Having this Accomplishment Do for You?

- *This gives me my life back; it gives me my family back. I feel like I am living in the modern world now, the present time. This is such a huge accomplishment for me. Accomplishing this shows me that I can do anything and everything I set my mind to. There is nothing that can be bigger than this. I am the victor! I did it!*

Step Eight – Positive Influences on Key Areas of Life

Relationships

- *My family is thrilled. They are so proud of me, and they eagerly snuggle up to me because I smell normal.*
- *I feel more confident about myself out in public, and so I am interacting with more people and finding it very pleasant to be pleasant.*
- *My confidence is rubbing off at work too. I feel perfectly comfortable being next to another person.*
- *My interactions now are more honest. I have nothing to hide, and I am free from any shame or embarrassment. I get to be me!*

> **Reframe** *so that the imagery created accurately reflects what is wanted.*
>
> *Reframe* **"and I am free from any shame or embarrassment"** *by removing the negative reference and replacing it with the desired outcome. For example,* **"confident and content"** *or deleted completely.*
>
> *Therefore, the entire reframed sentence would be:*

> *"My interactions now are honest. I have everything to show and share, and I am confident and content. I get to be me!"*

Career/Finances

- *Because my personal confidence has expanded, I am getting my work done more efficiently. I feel more approachable, more available, and more eligible for the promotion.*
- *Traveling for work is so easy now. The old panic about finding the time or a place to sneak a smoke is over, and those days are long gone! I am a respectable employee and proud of it!*

> **Reframe** *so that the imagery created accurately reflects what is wanted.*
>
> *Reframe* **"The old panic about finding the time or a place to sneak a smoke is over, and those days are long gone!"** *by removing the negative reference and replacing it with the desired outcome. For example,* **"The calmness about finding the time or a place to meditate or practice mindfulness is easy to find!"**

> *Therefore, the entire reframed sentence would be:*
>
> ***"Traveling for work is so easy now. The calmness about finding the time or a place to meditate or practice mindfulness is easy to find! I am a respectable employee and proud of it!"***

- *The money I have saved is a huge help to my family budget. It is like getting free utilities or a free car or vacation. And as the price of cigarettes goes up over time, so too do my savings. Getting a $300/month raise is something to be happy about.*

Health

- *I am grateful to be free from concern about getting lung cancer or mouth cancer.*

> **Reframe** *so that the imagery created accurately reflects what is wanted.*
>
> *Reframe* **"be free from concern about getting lung cancer or mouth cancer"** *by removing the negative reference and replacing it with the desired outcome. For example,* **"enjoy a healthy body from top to bottom."**

> *Therefore, the entire reframed sentence would be:*
>
> **"I am grateful to enjoy a healthy body from top to bottom."**

- *I am so happy to know that my body can repair a lot of the damage created by smoking.*

> **Reframe** *so that the imagery created accurately reflects what is wanted.*
>
> *Reframe* **"I am so happy to know that my body can repair a lot of the damage created from smoking"** *by removing the negative reference and replacing it with the desired outcome. For example,* **"that my body has been restored to good health."**
>
> *Therefore, the entire reframed sentence would be:*
>
> **"I am so happy knowing and feeling that my body has been restored to good health."**

- *Mentally and emotionally, I am thrilled to know I will be around for all the graduations, the weddings and to hold the newborn babies that come into our family.*

- *Because I am free from smoking, I find it easier to eat right and exercise regularly because now it matters! I can eat right and exercise, and it shows.*

> **Reframe** *so that the imagery created accurately reflects what is wanted.*
>
> *Reframe "***Because I am free from smoking***" by removing the negative reference and replacing it with the desired outcome.*
>
> *Therefore, the entire reframed sentence would be:*
>
> ***"I find it easier to eat right and exercise regularly because now it matters! I can eat right and exercise, and it shows."***

- *Because I am free from smoking, I am eating better and exercising, which translates into weight loss and better sleep! I am on a positive upward spiral now.*

> **Reframe** *so that the imagery created accurately reflects what is wanted.*
>
> *Reframe "***Because I am free from smoking***" by removing the negative reference and replacing it with the desired outcome.*

> *Therefore, the entire reframed sentence would be:*
>
> ***"I am eating better and exercising, which translates into weight loss and better sleep! I love being on a positive spiral!***

Self-Esteem

- *It feels so good to be free from beating myself up about smoking all the time. I was so mean to myself, and now I am so happy with myself!*

> ***Reframe*** *so that the imagery created accurately reflects what is wanted.*
>
> *Reframe* ***"It feels so good to be free from beating myself up about smoking all the time. I was so mean to myself"*** *by deleting the negative reference and replacing it with the desired outcome.*
>
> *Therefore, the entire reframed sentence would be,* ***"It feels so good to be so happy with myself!"***

- *It takes a lot to give up a habit like smoking, and I am very proud of this accomplishment.*

> **Reframe** *so that the imagery created accurately reflects what is wanted.*
>
> *Reframe* "**It takes a lot to give up a habit like smoking**" *by deleting the negative reference and replacing it with the desired outcome.*
>
> *Therefore, the entire reframed sentence would be,*" **I am very proud of this accomplishment!**

- *Living my life as a non-smoker makes me a better person in every part of my life. I really like who I am now. I am free to be me in every aspect.*

> **Reframe** *so that the imagery created accurately reflects what is wanted.*
>
> *Reframe* "**Living my life as a non-smoker**" *by deleting the negative reference and replacing it with the desired outcome.*
>
> *Therefore, the entire reframed sentence would be,*" **Living my life smoke-free makes me a better person in every part of my life. I really like who I am now. I am free to be me in every aspect.!**

Spirituality

- *I have a very strong spiritual practice. Now I can freely and confidently interact with those of like mind.*
- *The idea of going to a weeklong retreat is very appealing now.*
- *I have more time to spend on my spiritual studies.*
- *I have more money to spend on books, meditation CDs, and workshops related to my spiritual practice.*
- *I like the idea of creating a study group and having people over to my house. My house smells normal again, just like me.*

Conclusion

There you have it. You know everything you need to know about creating and perfecting a self-hypnosis practice to ensure optimal success in any part of your life. The only ingredient you need to add is the motivation and willingness to let this process take hold and create the neural pathways of practicing self-hypnosis regularly. You understand the value of repetition, so give this a shot, try it every day for ten days to two weeks, and then evaluate your progress.

If I could zero in on the most important things to remember regarding creating suggestions for your self-hypnosis, it would be to remember to use the words that create the imagery of what you want to have happen. Use the phrase, "Because I have accomplished [fill in the blank]," putting it in the present tense. If you phrase things in the future as something you are going to do or something you are working toward, you know that the changes you desire will always be the next big thing. I want you to make them the current big thing, right here and now in this present moment.

As you work through your Personal Change Blueprint, you will stimulate new ideas, so take your time. The more time you spend on it, the more details you will have to include in your session. Working through the Personal Change Blueprint is the most important part of the process.

In the middle of your self-hypnosis sessions, you will notice that other ideas related to your Personal Change Blueprint will come to mind. You will think of other changes that will occur because you have accomplished your outcome. Other ideas will come to mind regarding what your life will look like, sound like, or feel like. You will become aware of more positive influences on your career and finances, relationships, health, self-esteem, and spiritual practice right in the middle of your self-hypnosis session.

I always tell my clients that if new ideas come to mind while they are in the middle of hypnosis, that is fantastic. Just think those ideas right into the session. You are not limited to the details you wrote down when filling out your Personal Change Blueprint. Just make sure that the thoughts and images you are adding are thoughts and images of what you want to have happen.

I recommend keeping a journal of your progress. Document the areas of your life that you want to work on. Keep track of the changes you make and the evidence proving to yourself that you are learning and growing and expanding beyond where you have been. Take a moment to reflect back on the day each night before you drift off to sleep.

Acknowledge all that went right in the day. Acknowledge the baby steps and the quantum leaps, and know that you truly are in control of your life experiences every day. You have got this, and now you have an incredibly powerful tool in your toolbox. What do you want to start on first?

References

Laibow, R. (1999). Medical applications of neurobiofeedback. In J. R. Evans & A. Abarbanel (Eds.), *Introduction to quantitative EEG and neurofeedback* (pp. 83–102). Academic Press.

Self-Hypnosis for the 21ˢᵗ Century
Create Your Eight-Step Personal Change Blueprint

Debbie Taylor

debbietaylor-author.com

503-312-4660

Available to speak at your next event.

Connect with Debbie Taylor today!

www.ingramcontent.com/pod-product-compliance
Lightning Source LLC
Chambersburg PA
CBHW030038100526
44590CB00011B/258